Five Roads To Walleye

First printing 1997
Printed in the United States of America

Cover photo by Mari Romanack
Cover design by Print Masters
Interior layout and design by Kay Richey
Electronically created camera-ready copy by
KLR Communications, Inc.
POB 192
Grawn, MI 49637

Five Roads To Walleye By Mark Romanack
Walleye / Michigan - North America

ISBN

Acknowledgments

Where do I begin to say thank you? Thanking all the people who played a part in this book is no easy task. My knowledge of walleye fishing didn't form on its own, but rather from the influence of countless anglers with whom I've shared a boat. Fishing is a game you learn as you go. My ride on the walleye wave has been shared with many talented fishermen. Some are famous anglers and others just average guys, but they have all helped me become a better angler and outdoor communicator.

The physical look of this book is largely due to the talent and hard work of Kay Richey. The wife of Detroit News outdoor writer Dave Richey, Kay is an avid outdoor woman, computer wiz and talented book designer.

I'd also be remiss if I didn't thank some of the many manufacturers who's products I use frequently in the field. Companies like Champion Boats, Mercury Outboards, Off Shore Tackle, Riviera Downriggers, Lowrance Electronics, Stren Fishing Lines, Bait Rigs, Fred Arbogast Lures, Nautamatic Marine Systems, Storm Lures, Mustad Hooks, K&E Tackle, Warren Tackle Spinners, Luhr Jensen Fishing Tackle, Zebco and Quantum rods/reels, MotorGuide electric motors and dozens of others produce walleye fishing equipment that offers both function and value.

Five Roads To Walleye

By

Mark Romanack

Dedication

I always figured that after a couple books were under my belt the task of producing new titles would become easier. It hasn't. The fact is as my freelance magazine writing and photography business has become more successful, it has become harder to find the time required to research, write and finance outdoor books.

Ironically it's the outdoors itself that often gets in my way. My love of hunting and fishing and my resistance to give up those precious days spent outdoors has lead me to put Five Roads to Walleye on the back burner more times than I care to admit.

Alas, I know that writing books in addition to my regular freelance responsibilities requires that I spend less time in the field and longer hours at the computer. This in mind I willingly admit that Five Roads to Walleye would not have been possible without the support of my lovely wife Mari. In her unselfish way Mari motivates me to work harder, even though she knows that more hours in the office translates into less hours spent with the family.

In addition to being my personal motivator, Mari also runs interference at Outdoor Communications, taking phone calls, typing invoices, shipping books, running errands and about a million other behind the scenes tasks that make our day-to-day business run smoothly.

If it wasn't for Mari handling the jobs they don't give byline credit for, there wouldn't be enough time between magazine articles and photo shoots to attempt projects such as this my sixth book.

If all this wasn't enough Mari also takes loving care of our two boys Zackery and Jacob, seeing to it that Mom is always within earshot. I grew up with a Mom that played a similar role to Mari's. Call me old fashioned, but I believe kids thrive on this kind of stability.

To say I'm a lucky guy is a huge understatement. I've got everything in the world I want and I know enough to thank God and my loving wife Mari for that.

Contents

Pro-tips are highlighted in boxes within the chapters.

Ordering Information on page 200.

Introduction

Walleye are among the most unpredictable fish that swims. I've had the pleasure of catching walleye in less than 12 inches of water and more than 100 feet below the surface! In between I've found them belly to bottom on mud basins, scattered over sand flats, tucked up in dense patches of pond weed, hiding among the branches of fallen trees, suspended over open water, holding along rocky shorelines, poised on wing dams, living in river holes, waiting below the spillway of major dams, using main lake points, hovering above thermoclines, traveling along channel edges and making use of mid lake reefs just to name a few.

In my humble opinion walleye fishing is the ultimate fresh water angling challenge. If you catch a largemouth bass beneath a lily pad and let him go, the next day the same fish is likely to be waiting below the same lily pad.

Not so with walleye. Nomadic by nature, walleye are always on the go and not surprisingly tough to locate from day to day. These popular fish are a challenge to find even on fisheries that contain huge numbers of fish. Lake Erie is a perfect example. Over 50 million walleye are estimated to live in Lake Erie, yet there are many days I'd swear the lake was void of walleye. You've no doubt had similar experiences.

As compared to locating walleye, catching them is easy. For all practical purposes, there are only five major lure groups used to fish for walleye including jigs, live bait rigs, crankbaits, spoons and floats. Regardless of when or where walleye are found, one of these lure groups is the ideal method for catching them.It's from these basic five lure groups that this book title FIVE ROADS TO WALLEYE was conceived. To catch walleye you must travel down one or more of these five roads or paths. Frankly, the more lure groups and related presentations an angler masters the better his or her chances of consistently catching walleye becomes.

Sadly, most walleye anglers depend on one or two angling techniques. My company Outdoor Communications has a simple slogan that says it all. "Success begins with knowledge." Contained within these pages is the knowledge of how to catch walleye using all five primary lure groups. Each chapter contains several different presentation options, plus countless tips on tackle and equipment selection.

In addition to the straight forward and educational text you'll find dozens of pleasing photographs and illustrations that make the message of each chapter easier to understand. Digest the information contained in each chapter and then get out on the water and put your knowledge to work. Remember, walleye fishing success is as close as the knowledge in your hands.

Best fishes,

Mark Romanack

CHAMPION
Boats
CHAMPION

Casting Jigs

Jig casting appeals to many walleye anglers. For thousands of walleye enthusiasts the jig is the confidence lure they reach for both when hunting fish and for putting them in the boat. Many would argue that jigs rate as the all time favorite walleye fishing lure, and casting a jig tipped with a minnow, leech or piece of crawler certainly ranks as one of the most popular ways to catch walleye.

Despite the popularity of jigs and jig casting this presentation is one of the least understood and poorly practiced methods of walleye fishing. Lots of anglers enjoy casting leadheads, yet few do it well.

Unlike many other angling methods, jig casting requires a very specific list of equipment or "tools" that are must have items. The first item heading that list is a quality graphite spinning rod and reel combination. Graphite is the only material that is capable of telegraphing the light bites a walleye jig caster is likely to encounter.

Fiberglass and graphite/fiberglass composite rods simply can't get the job done effectively. At the very minimum select a rod that has 96% graphite content. The higher the percentage of graphite the more sensitive, light and responsive the rod becomes.

(Left) Mike Theyerl casted a Bait Rigs Slo-Poke jig to produce this walleye.

The length and action of a jig casting rod is also important. The best choices are 5'-6" to 6' models sporting a medium action. A jig casting rod must be fairly short and stiff. Longer or soft action rods tend to absorb much of the vibration or telegraphing effect of the rod.

For my money a rod featuring a Tennessee handle style is ideal. The smooth cork handle enables me to tape a spinning reel at exactly the point on the handle where it balances in my hand. Rods with fixed reel seats often make it impossible to balance the rod and reel. I simply use electrical tape to hold the reel securely.

The perfect reel for jig casting should be a light freshwater sized spinning reel. The new infinate anti-reverse reels available are the best possible choice. These reels have no slop in the reel handle, enabling the angler to deliver bone jaring hooksets. Once you've fished with one of these reels, going back to an ordinary spinning reel is out of the question.

The total jig casting rod and reel combination is likely to be the most expensive rod in your collection. Good rods range from $40-$100 and reels go for $50-$150 each. The good news is this combination should last the average angler a lifetime.

Fishing line is the next piece of essential equipment. Specificly I'm referring to monofilament. These days super braid lines are receiving a lot of attention and many anglers have mistakenly assumed that the new braided products are ideal for jig casting. They are not!

Braided lines have little or no stretch. When fishing these lines the angler can feel everything from the vibration of a blade to a jig dragging along the bottom. While it's nice to be able to feel what's happening on the end of the line, anglers must also realize that the ability to feel goes both ways.

Because the line doesn't stretch anglers can feel more of what's happening under water. In the same token, fish can feel the angler. What usually happens in this situation is the fish senses something is wrong, before the angler reacts to the bite and sets the hook. The result? Missed fish and lots of them.

Braided lines have lots of applications for walleye fishing, but based on my experience, jig casting isn't one of them. Monofilament is a better option for jig casting because it provides a moderate amount of stretch that enables the angler to feel bites without telegraphing anything unnatural to the fish.

Confused? Take an ordinary length of monofilament and pull on both ends. The line stretches like a rubber band. When the line is wet the stretch factor is even more pronounced. While this stretching of fishing line may seem counter productive it actually aids the angler who casts jigs or other fishing lures.

The stretch in monofilament makes it a little harder to feel the jig as it moves along bottom and it makes feeling bites a little more difficult, but with practice anyone can develop the skill or "feel" it takes to jig fish effectively. The key is learing to concentrate and fish the jig on a taunt line.

Before we get into jig casting techniques, we must first address a major problem associated with monofilament fishing lines. Memory. We've all seen fishing line memory. The tight coils of line that come off a reel that's been stored a long time is memory. Fishing with this stuff is like fishing with a slinky!

The coils in the line make it impossible to keep a taunt line between rod tip and lure. In fact, memory coils provide enough slack line that a fish can pick up the bait and swim away with it without the angler ever knowing it. Remember this, you can't feel the bite if there is slack in the line. IF THERE IS SLACK IN THE LINE YOU CAN'T FEEL THE BITE. I repeated myself because this simple fact of jig fishing is where most folks go wrong.

Using monofilament with low or no memory is the first step towards keeping the line taunt. My choice is Stren's new Easy Cast in six or eight pound test. This copolymer line is designed to have a soft surface that resists coiling and comes off the reel smoothly. I use the lighter line most of the time, but keep some eight pound test handy when fishing in weeds, timber or broken

A raised front deck is the ideal place to cast jigs. Note this angler is using a foot controlled electric motor to control the boat.

rock where snags are a fact of fishing.

Equipped with the right rod, reel and monofilament fishing line, an angler can approach jig casting seriously. Also, armed with the knowledge that to feel the bite the line must be kept taunt as much as possible, gives the angler a mind set of what must be done to achieve jig casting success.

Here's were the concentration part comes into play. Keeping tension or a tauntness in the line requires a concious effort on the part of the angler. Casting a jig and working it properly back to the boat or your shore position isn't difficult, but it does require a meeting of the mind and body.

I'm not talking about jig casting according to ZEN, I'm talking about a simple procedure that makes jig casting something any angler can master.

Start out by making a short to moderate cast. Long casts are difficult to control and should be avoided. In most instances jig casting is a shallow water game. I primarily use this technique when fishing in water from a foot or two deep out to about 10-12 feet.

Short shank jigs are ideal for casting when tipped with live bait.

At these depths a 1/16 or 1/8 ounce jig is the standard weapon. My personal choice is a short shank live bait style jig such as the Bait Rigs Slo-Poke. This eye forward jig is ideal for working through weeds, rock and wood with the least amount of hang-ups. Live bait style jigs also feature a wider hook gap than other jig styles making them good hookers.

If the wind is blowing it may be in your best interest to use a slightly heavier jig such as a 3/16 or 1/4 ounce model. Heavier jigs are easier to feel on bottom and the angler has a better chance to keep bow out of the line caused by the wind picking up the monofilament. Bow in the line has the same effect as slack, making it impossible to feel bites.

Let the jig sink to bottom by keeping the reel bait open until the line collapses and lays still on the surface. Close the reel bail and face directly at the jig. Hold the rod in the 10 o'clock position and slowly reel up the slack line until the weight of the jig can be felt resting on bottom.

When the line comes taunt pull the rod from the 10 o'clock position to the 11 o'clock position and hold the rod still for a few seconds. This rod motion pulls the jig slightly off bottom and causes the jig to pendulem towards you on a taunt line. When the jig hits bottom again the line will go slack on the surface. Reel down to the 10 o'clock position again picking up the slack line in the process and repeat the procedure. That's it. Over and over again work the rod from 10 o'clock to 11 o'clock and concentrate on keeping the line taunt.

Your point of focus should be the point where the line enters the water. Line watching is a step towards increasing your concentration skills and it helps the angler to visualize what it takes to keep a taunt line. Also, watching the line provides a different education. Many bites aren't felt, but can be seen when the line twitches or darts sideways.

If you have excellent eye sight and can easily see clear, green or brown color monofilaments I'd recommend using them. On bright days a pair of sunglasses makes this chore much easier. However anglers who suffer from poor eye sight should consider using the fluorscent lines on the market. Stren's Clear Blue is is my personal choice, but there are other good products out there.

If the water is cloudy or slightly off color I've never seen brightly colored lines make any difference in the number of bites. However if the water is gin clear, I'd stay away from lines that are so bright they almost seem to glow. The manufacturers of these lines say their products are highly visible above water and invisible underwater. I know of many scuba divers that say differently. In fact when we test crankbaits for various updated versions of the book Precision Trolling, we use fluorescent lines so we can see the lures under water more easily. Think about it.

Another mistake that many jig fishermen make is to reel in their lure and cast again before working the bait all the way back to the boat. Don't be impatient. Walleye are like northern pike. They often follow a lure or bait, waiting for the last possible second before striking. If you get in a hurry and reel in before the jig is worked all the way to the boat, you could be missing fish.

When you're doing everything right and a walleye bites your jig, the sensation you feel at the other end of the line isn't exactly overwhelming. In fact, many people have a hard time even detecting the difference between a bite and the jig hitting something under water. All I can tell you is that the bite will feel like a sharp tick or tap in the line and once you've felt it you'll know what I'm talking about.

In the jig casting game there aren't any smashing strikes. If that's what you want to feel, cast a crankbait, spoon or spinner. These faster moving lures are typically attacked more aggressively. When a walleye hits a jig and minnow combination, he simply slurps it into his mouth and swims off to eat his meal. Unless you concentrate, the whole deal could pass you by.

No jig casting chapter would be complete without a few words on live bait choices. Minnows, leeches and crawlers can all be used effectively for jig casting. The use of these baits tends to be seasonal. Minnows are more readily available in the spring and fall. Crawlers and leeches fill in during the warm water months. All work equally well.

When casting minnows, I lean towards fatheads, chubs, dace or small suckers. These species stay on a hook better and live longer than emerald shiners, golden shiners and other delicate minnows. Many times I've visited bodies of water where local anglers say you have to fish a particular type of minnow or the walleye won't bite. Horse apples!

The first time I fished a tournament on Lake Erie the only minnows available were small emerald shiners. The bait shops and local anglers stood on soap boxes and argued that shiners were the only minnow that would work.

I called a friend in Wisconsin who runs a bait shop and ordered a pound of fatheads and had him air ship the bait to me UPS overnight. The next day I was catching walleye with minnows that stay on the hook and wiggle twice as long. During the tournament my daily pro partners turned up their noses at my bait choice until they saw how many walleye I could catch. The moral of the story, use a minnow that stays on the hook.

When casting crawlers I usually break the bait in half and thread one half onto the hook like you might thread a plastic grub onto a jig. Casting half a crawler works. It doesn't look like much, but it works.

In some cases I favor casting with plastic over live bait. Scented plastic grubs like Power Bait and Reaction Lures are powerful fish catching tools. In areas where it's tough to get bait, such as on fly-in trips to Canada, I always go prepared with scent impregnated soft plastics. I've even seen these products out fish live bait at times.

A final aspect of jig casting deals with the hookset. He who hesitates is lost! Set the hook the second you feel anything. This hard and fast rule of jig fishing applies across the board. When fishing a jig you never hesitate or attempt to feed line to the fish. Hit him now and hit him with a strong rod sweep that takes up slack line and line stretch as much as possible.

In my business I'm forever rehooking fish so I can take photographs. Putting a jig hook securely into a walleye's mouth takes a pair of pliers. The hard bone and tissue around a walleye's jaw is very difficult to put a hook into. That's why I use jigs with thin wire hooks that are as sharp as possible. A thin wire hook is easier to bury to the barb than a larger tempered style hook.

If you watch while I'm casting jigs you'll often see me set the hook by raising my arms high over my head. Sometimes I even stand. Standing helps to pick up slack and line stretch and makes it easier to keep solid pressure on the fish.

When fishing light line and jigs you can't hit the fish hard enough at the hookset to drive the hook past the barb. If you set the hook that hard the line would likely break. Instead you simply use a rapid rod sweep to put pressure on the fish. When the fish thrashes to rid itself of the jig, his side to side movement helps the hook point work its way into the flesh and bone.

Like any other type of fishing, becoming a successful jig fisherman isn't a stroke of magic. A simple set of tools and techniques are needed to make jig casting one of your most effective and enjoyable walleye fishing techniques.

In the next chapter we'll discuss jig dragging. A slightly different presentation than jig casting, this fishing method is the easiest of all jig fishing techniques to learn and master.

CHAPTER TIPS

1. Light line is critical to jig casting success. Six pound test is the best all around size, however some situations may call for four or eight pound test.

2. Any jig can be cast, but short shank live bait style jigs are among the best option.

3. Jig casting is a shallow water game. For best results concentrate on waters 12 feet deep or less.

4. Graphite is the only suitable material for a jig casting rod. High quality graphite rods are expensive, but they are also lightweight, sensitive and best able to telegraph the light strikes typical of jig casting.

Chapter 2

Dragging Jigs

Sometimes things are as they seem. In the case of jig dragging, what you see is what you get. This simple presentation is based on slowly dragging the jig along bottom. Obviously, this is a presentation that works best on sand, gravel or clay bottoms. If the bottom is covered with snags, dragging a jig is likely to yield more headaches than walleye.

Not only is dragging a highly effective jigging presentation, this simple angling method is easy for anyone to master. In fact, this is the most basic of all jigging styles.

The tools used for jig dragging vary somewhat as compared to jig casting. Since the rod is positioned in a holder or leaning up against the gunwales of the boat much of the time, there is no need to use expensive graphite rods. Graphite makes for an excellent jig dragging rod, but to be honest a less expensive fiberglass or graphite/fiberglass composite rod would accomplish the same goal with less cash layout.

The rods I use for jig dragging also double as slip sinker rigging and slip bobber rods. My preference are 6' to 6'-6" graphite rods with a medium/light or light action.

I match these rods up with a light freshwater spinning reel

(left) Ken Ellis of Green Bay Wisconsin is a master jig fisherman. This dandy pre-spawn fish was caught by slowly dragging a jig along bottom.

and six pound test green Stren. Green line is the least visible in the water and since dragging jigs doesn't require the angler to line watch, a low visibility line makes sense.

If the area to be fished produces a fair number of snags, bumping up to eight pound test will help salvage a few jigs that might otherwise be lost to the bottom. When using heavier line the wire hook on the jig can often be bent out and the jig recovered. Simply bend the hook back into shape, sharpen the hook, rebait and start over.

The jigs used for dragging presentation can vary. Stand-up style jigs including such favorites as the Bait Rigs Odd Ball and Slo-Up jig are popular with many anglers. These jig designs position the hook upright off the bottom where the bait is more visible plus this hook position helps to keep snags to a minimum.

Standard round ball style jigs can also be dragged effectively. Eye forward jigs such as the Slo-Poke are another good jig dragging choice. In jig dragging the style of the jighead is less important than in other jigging methods. What's important is the hook used on the jig. For best results the hook should be made of thin wire.

A thin wire hook will penetrate and hold better than hooks made from thicker materials. Think of it this way; a ball point pen could be pushed through a piece of paper with a little force, but a straight pin would pierce the same paper with much less force. Thin wire hooks accomplish the same goal and are a good choice in most jig fishing situations.

WHERE TO DRAG JIGS

Jigs can be dragged in a wealth of walleye fishing situations. River flats are one of my favorite places to drag jigs during the post-spawn period when walleye are looking for easy meals. The best rivers are those that feature a slow to moderate current flow. Across walleye wonderland there are more of these streams than you can shake a jigging stick at.

The methodology is simple, relaxing and amazingly effective. In rivers walleye tend to spread out on large flats. Because

Leon Houle used a light action spinning rod, six pound test line and a 1/8 ounce jig to produce this summer walleye.

the current flow is reduced in these flats, walleye can lay in the current for hours waiting for food to be washed within reach.

Drifting downstream and dragging jigs is a great way to fish these flats because it covers water quickly, throughly and presents the bait in a natural manner to waiting walleye.

When setting up to drag a flat, motor well above the area to be fished and turn the boat sideways to the current. Depending on the wind direction it may be necessary to occasionally use an electric motor to keep the boat drifting sideways. It's important to keep the boat positioned sideways to maximize the bottom coverage and to prevent lines from crossing and getting tangled.

A minnow, crawler or leech may be used for bait. Although I can't explain why, a whole nightcrawler hooked through the collar is one of the best baits for jig dragging in rivers. I've taken countless walleye with this jig/live bait option and I've learned not to question why. It just works.

However, the smart move is to take all three live baits along and experiment to see which one the fish prefer. When the boat starts drifting downstream cast the jig upstream and allow it to sink to bottom. The drifting boat will soon pull the line tight and start dragging the jig along the bottom.

You should be able to feel the jig as it slides along the bottom. In most cases a 1/16 or 1/8 ounce jig is ideal. Once you're sure the jig is dragging along the bottom nicely, the rod can be held, placed in a rod holder or simply leaned up against the side of the boat.

This style of fishing is an ideal opportunity to fish a second line where legal. Most anglers hold one rod and let the second rest in a rod holder. Ironically, it's the rod that's not attended that often produces the most bites.

There's no logical reason why a rod in a holder would out fish one held in your hands, but I've seen in happen enough not to question this phenomenon. My advice is to fish two rods and let at least one sit motionless in a holder.

When the boat is drifting and the jigs sliding along bottom the rod tips tap out a rythmic motion. When a fish picks up the bait, the rod simply feels heavy and the tip starts to bend from the weight of the fish.

As in all styles of jigging, set the hook immediately with a strong upwards rod sweep. Fight the fish to net, toss it on ice, bait up and get back in the water.

Most of the fish caught along these river flats are post-spawn males that range from 15-18 inches long or in other words the perfect size for fish sandwiches! This spring pattern is an excellent way to put a few welcome fillets in the freezer.

When fish are located, make repeated drifts over the most productive areas. In addition to walleye, this simple fishing method is likely to yield catfish, smallmouth, carp and drum. The action is often fast paced and always a good time.

Another favorite jig dragging pattern takes place in natural lakes during the spring and early summer. After spawning, natural lake walleye head for areas of the lake that are often referred to as food shelves. Typically these areas are shallow water flats, reefs and bars that warm quickly and in turn attract baitfish. Baitfish instinctively head to shallow water to take advantage of the blooming plankton levels. Walleye being opportunistic creatures invade the shallows to feed on this food bonanza.

Ideal areas are locations where the water runs from six to 15 feet deep. If walleye are located in shallower water, jig casting is usually a more effective presentation. If the fish are found deeper, jig trolling becomes a more controlled and effective fishing method.

Dragging jigs in these areas is similar to dragging in rivers except it's the wind not current that provides the boat motion. If there is no wind, an electric motor can be used to slowly drag jigs along the bottom. Using an electric motor to drag jigs is something we'll detail in the chapter Jig Trolling.

Position the boat upwind of the area to be fished and set up the same way as when drifting jigs in rivers. Depending on water

Ted Takasaki often uses a small gasoline kicker to control his boat while dragging jigs.

depth and the force of the wind, it may be necessary to use slightly heavier jigs. A selection of 1/8, 3/16 and 1/4 ounce leadheads should cover any jig dragging situation.

A set of sea anchors is a must have item for this style of fishing. Designed to control drifting speed, I recommend using two moderately sized bags as opposed to one large bag. Using two bags gives the angler more flexibility to control drifting speed as necessary.

The bags I've been using for years are 40-inches in diameter and made from ripstop nylon that's lightweight and dries quickly. I rig my bags with two ropes, one on the front of the bag and a second line attached to the rear of the bag to make pulling them in easier. If a sea anchor only has one rope attached, pulling it in can be back breaking work.

When using a single bag I attach it to the middle of the boat. Hooked fish are fought and landed on either end of the boat. When the wind blows a little harder, I use two bags and position one near the bow and the other near the stern. Hooked fish are brought to and landed in the middle of the boat.

If you do a lot of drift fishing and use sea anchors frequently, I recommend purchasing tie down cleats and mounting them in convenient locations. A cleat is the ideal and safest way to attach a sea bag.

Another important accessory are several marker buoys. When a fish is hooked toss out a marker and make another drift over the area. Be sure when setting up to make another drift that you motor around the area you plan to fish. Running an outboard over top of the area to be fished is the fastest way I know to kill a walleye bite.

Most marker buoys are yellow in color. Yellow can be tough to see, especially on gray or overcast days. I paint my markers flame red so I can see them. Unfortunately, so can other anglers. More than once I've had anglers move in on my markers. Even more disturbing, I've had my markers picked up and stolen while I was still fishing! There's no accounting for what some folks will do.

I also take the thin twine that comes on most markers and replace it with heavy decoy anchor cord. The heavier cord is easier to wrap and it tangles much less. You need at least two or three markers for serious jig dragging.

Jig dragging isn't fancy and that's what appeals to many anglers. Walleye fishing doesn't have to be a drag, but sometimes it's the best way to fill a limit.

In the next chapter we'll discuss one of the most popular river fishing techniques, vertical jigging.

CHAPTER TIPS

1. Rod holders are a valuable boat accessory when dragging jigs. If the price on rod holders looks too good to be true it probably is. Quality rod holders start at around $20.00.

2. When dragging a jig tipped with a whole nightcrawler, hook the crawler through the collar. If only a piece of crawler is used, thread the bait onto the hook like a plastic grub body.

3. Minnows and leeches also make excellent live baits for jig dragging.

4. Just about any rod and reel can be used to drag jigs. Push button style reels are a good choice, especially among youngsters and others just learning how to fish. Spinning tackle is the all around best choice for jig dragging.

5. Jig dragging works especially well in rivers, but this simple fishing method can also be used effectively in both large and small lakes.

6. Where legal, use two rods when dragging jigs. The extra line can double your chances of catching fish.

Chapter 3

Vertical Jigging

Up, down, up, down, up, down. Vertical jigging doesn't seem very difficult. After all, how tough can it be to lift a jig up off bottom and then set it back down again? Vertical jigging is one of the most common ways to fish walleye in rivers, yet there's more to this common presentation than meets the eye. What the casual angler doesn't see is the dynamics between the flowing water, lure and boat. To vertical jig effectively the boat, current and jig must all drift along at the same speed.

In a perfect world, drifting in river current and fishing a jig directly beneath the boat would be easy. Unfortunately, the world is far from perfect and staying vertical is anything but easy.

The wind is what makes vertical jigging a challenge. When the wind blows it turns an ordinary walleye boat into a sail boat and one of two things usually happens. Either the wind pushes the boat downstream faster than the current or the wind prevents the boat from drifting as fast as the flowing water.

When the boat moves faster than the current the line sharply angles upstream. If the wind blows against the current, the boat's drifting speed becomes slower than the current and the jig gets swept downstream of the boat. Either way, the vertical presenta-

(Left) Keith Lutz is a talented taxidermist and expert river fisherman. This walleye was taken by vertical jigging on the Saginaw River during December.

tion is lost making it difficult to maintain contact with the bottom.

When it comes to the delicate art of vertical jigging, presentation is everything. The jig must be kept close to the bottom to interest walleye that hold tight to bottom to avoid being washed away with the current. Also, staying vertical makes it easier to present a jig tight to bottom without running the risk of dragging and snagging up.

Unlike other forms of walleye fishing where your presentation can be a little sloppy and still function, vertical jigging requires a higher degree of boat control and personal concentration. The line must be vertical, the jig must be close to but not on bottom and the boat must be constantly controlled to keep it that way.

The best way to control a boat while vertical jigging is with a foot controlled bow mounted electric motor. From the bow of the boat an angler has the best leverage to move the boat as needed. It's much easier to move the pointed bow end of the boat in the water than the flat transom.

When two anglers are fishing, the best place to stand is on the front casting deck. When vertical jigging the back of the boat constantly swings back and forth as the person controlling the boat uses the electric motor to keep his line vertical. It's easier to stay vertical when fishing near the front of the boat.

A foot controlled motor also allows the angler to keep both hands free making it possible to fish two rods. With a little practice, two rod jigging is a sure way to double your vertical jigging success.

Here's a tip that makes two rod jigging easier to master. When one rod needs to be baited or a new jig tied on, place the second rod in a holder that positions the rod tip straight up. Resting in this position the jig is off bottom and won't snag while you're busy working on another rod. Once both rods are baited and ready to go, let the jigs down to bottom and work both rods using the same jigging cadence.

Keith Kavajecz demonstrates the art of two rod jigging. Where allowed, using two rods doubles the angler's chances of contacting fish and makes it easier to experiment with color and bait options.

When vertical jigging remember that it's difficult to position the jig under the boat, but the boat can easily be positioned over top of the jig. This is accomplished by simply moving the boat in whatever direction is needed to keep the boat drifting at the same speed as the current. Start out by pointing the bow of the boat into the wind and using short bursts of power from the electric motor to keep the boat, jig and current all moving along at the same speed.

At first most anglers tend to use too much power from the electric motor. When too much power is used the boat moves towards the vertical position then momentum carries it beyond the vertical point. With a little practice, the art of vertical jigging or what is sometimes called chasing the line, becomes second nature.

When learning the basics of vertical jigging it helps to use a fairly heavy jig. Once your skills sharpen, use progressively lighter jigs that are easier for walleye to inhale into their mouth.

Once the basic boat control chores involved in vertical jigging are mastered, equipment should become a primary focus.

Rods should be considered a critical part of vertical jigging. A good vertical jigging rod should be a short (5.5 to 6 feet long) spinning model with a stiff action.

I actually cut an inch or two off the tip of my jigging rods to make them a little stiffer and more sensitive jigging tools. When you cut off a jigging rod be sure to add a new tip top guide and epoxy it into place.

A light freshwater spinning reel is the best match for this rod. I personally favor the new continuous anti-reverse reels that have no slop or play in the handle. This simple feature makes setting the hook a more direct and positive experience.

Line is another important jigging tool. For most vertical jigging situations six pound test is ideal. I personally favor a low memory line such as Stren Easy Cast. This soft surfaced line slips off the reel spool smoothly and without the annoying coil or memory present in most lines.

The jigs used can also be important. Jigs with long shank wire hooks are the best hookers because the hook point reaches a little further into the walleye's mouth and the thin wire penetrates with less effort.

The head can be many different shapes, but the line tie needs to come out the top of the jig so the bait hangs horizontal in the water. Round ball and darter style heads are my favorites for vertical jigging. I also like a jig that features a second eyelet for attaching a stinger hook. There are many excellent jigs on the market with this feature.

A stinger hook is a must item if minnows are the bait used for vertical jigging. If crawlers or leeches are used, a stinger hook simply balls up in the bait and reduces natural action.

Many anglers say that using a stinger is more trouble (they seem to hook on everything in the boat) than good. I couldn't disagree more. The effort required to fish stingers more than pays for itself. If the fish are biting light, a stinger hook could easily produce 40% more fish a day.

Stingers or cheaters are critical to vertical jigging success. This walleye would have been another one that got away if it wasn't for the use of a stinger hook.

Stinger hooks work best when they are tied using eight or 10 pound test monofilament and round bend style No. 10 treble hooks. The ideal length seems to be about four to five inches. Stingers made from steel leader material are stiff and can impart a mechanical action to the jig-n-minnow presentation. Stick with stingers tied on monofilament. Both commercially tied and homemade versions are effective.

Whether you use a stinger hook or not, always set the hook the instant a bite is felt. When jig fishing you never feed a fish line, lower your rod tip before setting the hook or for any reason delay in setting the hook. To do so is inviting the walleye to drop the bait. In jig fishing he who hesitates is truly lost.

Dressing a jig with a soft plastic body also makes sense. Using plastic helps to bulk up the bait so it becomes easier to spot in turbid waters. Also, grub bodies can add action, scent and even taste to the presentation.

Almost any grub tail can be used for vertical jigging, but twister style grubs are hands down the most popular among walleye anglers. Twister style grubs are designed to provide action even if the jig is tipped with a live minnow.

Scented and taste impregnated grubs such as Reaction Lures and Power Bait are outstanding choices for walleye fishing. These products encourage walleye to strike and hang onto the bait longer.

When choosing jig and grub colors let common sense and water clarity be a guideline. I like natural shades that closely resemble available forage when the water is clear. In stained or dirty water progressively brighter colors are easier to see and produce better.

A trick I learned from a bass angler many years ago makes fishing with plastic grubs easier. Place a drop of Super Glue on the jig collar just before threading on the plastic body. Once the grub is pushed into position, the glue dries quickly and holds the grub firmly in place. A great way to fish plastic, rigged in this manner the body stays put even after catching several fish.

Predicting where fish will be located is another vital aspect of vertical jig fishing. Walleye in rivers are always on the move, but one common thread makes their whereabouts predicable. Experienced river rats look for slack water. Any place the force of the current is interrupted, walleye are likely to concentrate. Collectively known as current breaks, finding these areas is the key to fishing success.

Some typical current breaks include large flats where the river widens and the current slows down, subtle depressions in the bottom, deep holes and outside bends in the river and eddies formed where points or downed timber interrupt the current flow. These areas are just a few of the places to seek out river run walleye.

A good vertical jigging drift may only be a few yards long or a 1/4 mile. When fish are located, note the water depth and take a shoreline sighting. By making additional drifts over the same water, large numbers of fish can be cherry picked from prime spots. Remember, when running back upstream to set up another drift, be sure not to motor over top of the area to be fished.

Also, it doesn't hurt to make a few notes regarding the locations of fish in a log book. River walleye show up in specific places for specific reasons. A spot that holds fish today is likely to attract fish again and again. Once an angler has located a number of these fish producing spots, each new day on the water simply becomes a milk run that leads the angler from spot to spot.

Vertical jigging works best in water from six to 30 feet deep. When fishing shallow water a 1/16 or 1/8 ounce jig is ideal. To handle progressively deeper water 3/16, 1/4, 3/8, 1/2 and 5/8 ounce jigs may be required.

Ideally an angler should select the lightest jig that can be easily felt contacting bottom. However, it's better to use a slightly heavier jig and have perfect presentation, than to struggle with a jig that's too light and difficult to feel hitting bottom.

Jigging action is the final concern a vertical jigger must be aware of. There are no limits to the jigging variations vertical jiggers use. The important thing is to change jigging strokes or cadence until a successful pattern develops, then concentrate on that pattern.

A couple simple jigging strokes will get you started in the right direction. One of my most productive vertical jigging strokes is something I call tight line jigging. The jig is raised and dropped slowly, keeping tension or a tauntness in the line at all times. This simple stroke works especially well in cold water when fish are inactive.

Another excellent jigging stroke incorporates a slow tight line lift followed by a rapid dropping of the rod tip that allows the jig to free fall back to bottom. With all vertical jigging styles the jig shouldn't be raised more than a few inches off bottom.

You may find these jigging strokes work wonders, or that your own inventions work better. The important thing is to stay vertical, concentrate and set the hook immediately.

Presentation is the name of the game when it comes to vertical jigging. Those who master this unique form of river drift fishing are often rewarded with huge catches of fish and trophy fish to boot. When I give seminars on vertical jigging, folks are often amazed at how technical this fishing presentation can be. To those anglers who are resistant to learning the tricks of vertical jigging, I'm quick to point out there are easier ways to catch walleye but none as effective.

In the next chapter we'll visit a form of jigging that combines the traditional forms of jigging with a trolling slant. The result is a jigging presentation that simply vacuums up walleye living along defined bottom structure.

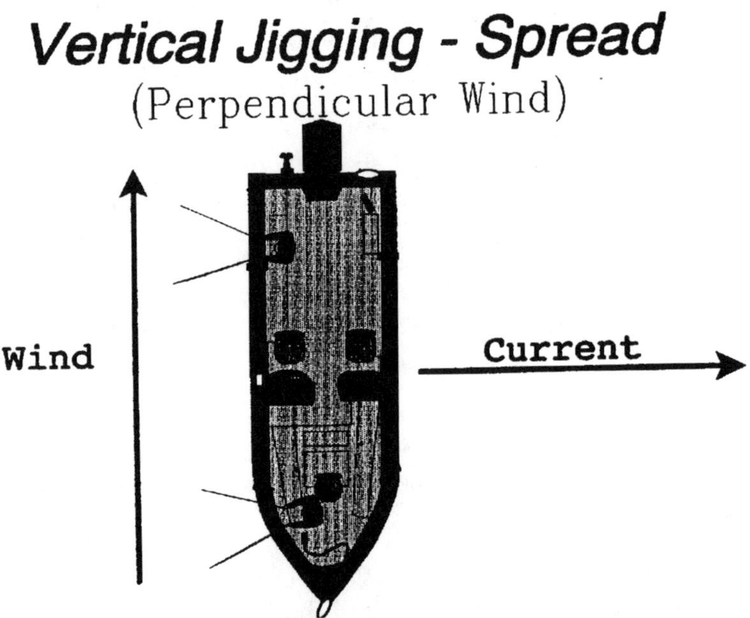

When vertical jigging the boat is controlled by moving it over top of the jig in an effort to make the boat and jig drift downstream at the same speed.

CHAPTER TIPS

1. Long shank jigs are ideal for vertical jigging. The extra hook shank makes it easy to add plastic bodies and positions the hook point a little deeper in the mouth of walleyes that bite.

2. When vertical jigging with two lines, never lay down one rod when baiting or tying on a new jig. Always reel up the second line to avoid snags or better yet, position the rod in a rod holder with the tip pointed straight up. Positioned in this manner, the second line won't snag while a different line is being tended.

3. When vertical jigging it's best to use a jig that's a little too heavy than one that's too light. In shallow water 1/8 and 1/4 ounce jigs are the norm, while 3/8 and 1/2 ounce jigs may be needed to fish deeper waters.

4. A stinger hook should be standard equipment when vertical jigging. Stinger hooks can be purchased or you can tie your own using eight or 10 pound test monofilament and No. 10 treble hooks.

5. An electric motor is a "must have" item for vertical jigging. A bow mount motor is the best choice, but transom mounted motors can also be used to vertical jig.

6. A short stiff rod works best for vertical jigging. Many anglers make their rods stiffer by simply cutting a couple inches off the tip and installing a new tip top guide.

Chapter 4

Jig Trolling

Are jigs the ultimate weapon for catching walleye? Simply stated, it's awfully hard to find another lure that's as versatile, effective and as readily available.

If jigging has a downfall, it's that this popular angling presentation is time consuming. Casting to sunken tree tops, hopping a leadhead along a rock strewn bottom or pitching jigs along weed edges are slow and methodical ways to fish. In fact, most jigging techniques eat up the clock too fast to be considered valuable fish finding tactics.

Locating fish takes time without the added burden of slow paced presentations. That's exactly why experienced anglers favor angling methods that quickly eliminate unproductive water.

WHY TROLL JIGS?

For structure or bottom orientated fish, a jig is a tough lure to improve upon. When it comes to fishing efficiently, slow trolling and bumping a jig along bottom is a hard presentation to beat.

Jig trolling is best described as a fish harvesting system. Designed to be fast paced, thorough and versatile enough to apply to a wide variety of angling situations, combining jigs and trolling makes sense.

(Left) Dale Voice enjoys jig fishing in all its forms. This beauty came from the lower Detroit River where it drains into Lake Erie.

Effective on walleye and many other species, jigs can be trolled along shorelines or open water structure that features gravel, sand, clay or scattered rock bottoms. Jigs can also be trolled along weed edges, meandering breaks and on flats.

Some of the most productive jig trolling applications exist where large flats need to be covered or meandering edges and bottom contours must be followed. This unique angling technique really shines when working bottom contour lines, weed edges, creek channels, saddles between reefs and other areas where fish tend to be scattered.

Most serious anglers already have the right tools to troll jigs. Jig trolling requires a boat equipped with an electric motor and or small gasoline kicker motor, dependable fishing sonar, sensitive graphite rods and an assortment of leadhead jigs complete with plastic grub bodies and an assortment of live bait.

A bow mounted electric motor equipped with a foot control, constant on and variable speed control functions is a good choice for boat control when fishing in shallow water, very clear water or if the water surface is calm. In rougher water, stained conditions or when fishing deep water a kicker motor is a more efficient tool for jig trolling.

Powerful 24 volt motors are the best choice for boats ranging in size from 17 to 20 foot. These high output electrics generate the whopping 40 to 60 pounds of thrust it takes to control large boats in strong winds and waves. Smaller boats can get by with 12 volt electric motors that feature 28 to 36 pounds of thrust. For maximum power, anglers may want to consider the 36 volt electric motors on the market. Designed to tie into the existing cranking battery to add extra bursts of power when needed, these products currently represent the strongest electric motors available.

When choosing a gasoline kicker, sizes ranging from six to 15 horsepower are best. Models that generate 9.9 and 15 hp respectively are the most popular with walleye anglers.

A new product designed to aid in boat control was designed to fit on most models of gasoline kickers. The Nautamatic TR-1 auto-pilot is a one of a kind product. An electronic compass and small hydraulic cylinder are used to keep the boat on course in wind, waves and even current.

When the bow of the boat moves the compass senses the change in course and sends a message to the hydraulic cylinder to move the motor accordingly. Fast and responsive, the TR-1 is controlled by a simple forward and reverse switch and a hand-held remote that is used to change course headings. Owners of four stroke outboards can also purchase a throttle control that allows both the boat's heading and speed to be maintained from a single remote control.

This unique auto-pilot can be interfaced with any standard Loran-C or GPS unit for even more convenience. For more information regarding the TR-1 call 1-800-588-7655.

In addition to a boat equipped with an electric motor and or kicker a good assortment of leadhead jigs in sizes ranging from 1/8 to 5/8 ounce are required equipment. Sensitive graphite spinning and baitcasting outfits and plenty of premium monofilament, plus plastic grub bodies, stinger hooks and a good selection of lively crawlers, leeches and minnows are mandatory items.

TEAM WORK IS IMPORTANT

Jig trolling is most efficient when a pair of anglers work as a team. Both anglers should fish two (where legal) rods to maximize lure coverage. The angler who controls the boat is the key to the system. This angler must interpret the sonar and use depth data to keep the boat on course.

Liquid Crystal Readout, video and paper graphs take a few seconds to interpret data received from the transducer and print it out on the screen in a form anglers can understand. This brief delay in data transmission is enough time to let the boat drift slightly off course.

Sonar units like Lowrance's X-75 and X-85 feature both a digital depth reading and two dimensional bottom display. Subtle changes in depth are indicated instantly on the digital depth reading, making it easy to anticipate boat control moves seconds before the two dimensional screen confirms changes in bottom contour.

Gary Parsons demonstrates the art of jig trolling. Note he is using a liquid crystal graph to keep on course and a foot controlled electric motor to move the boat. Using two rods doubles the chances of contacting fish.

The graph should be mounted in clear view of the angler operating the boat. From this position the angler can observe the graph while maintaining boat control.

The angler in charge of boat control must also determine and maintain the best trolling speed. Ideally the boat should be moving at a speed that eats up water, but allows the jigs to contact the bottom.

Jig trolling works best in water from 6 to 20 feet deep. In shallow water, the boat may spook fish before the lures have a chance to do their job. In deeper water it becomes difficult to maintain bottom contact.

The man controlling the boat selects heavy jigs that can be fished at about a 45 degree angle under the boat. It's important to keep this angler's jigs as vertical as possible to avoid the line becoming tangled in the second angler's lines. Depending on water depth and boat speed it usually takes a 3/8 to 5/8 ounce jig to stay in contact with bottom.

Meanwhile the second angler fishes with a lighter jig. Normally a 1/8 or 1/4 ounce jig is the best choice. Keeping the lighter jigs on bottom forces the second angler to let out a lot more line. The added lead length prevents the two anglers from tangling their lines and provides a different look and action to the jigs as they move along bottom.

The angler controlling the boat often catches most of the fish. Active fish are prone to hit the first presentation that passes them. However, there are days when the angler who fishes the lighter jigs cleans house. If one presentation is clearly better, take turns sharing the most productive technique.

JIGS & JIG DRESSINGS

Almost any combination of leadhead jigs, plastic grub bodies or live bait jig dressings can be used effectively while trolling jigs. Leadheads that feature long shank wire hooks are best. Long shank hooks help to reach back into the bony mouth of walleye a little better than jigs with short shank hooks.

Thin diameter wire hooks also penetrate bone easier than heavy tempered steel hooks. Wire hooks have the advantage of being soft enough to bend out if the hook should snag on bottom. By applying steady pressure, the hook can be bent out and many jigs saved that would otherwise be donated to the lake bottom.

Jigs should also feature a barbed collar that helps hold plastic grubs in place on the hook shank. Plastic grubs can also be glued in place to prevent them from sliding down the hook shank when a fish is caught.

Thread the grub body onto the jig hook and put a drop of Super Glue on the jig collar before pushing the plastic body tight against the head. Let the glue dry for a few moments before using the lure.

A variety of jighead designs can be used for trolling effectively. The standard ball style head is an excellent choice. Stand-up jigs give the bait a different look and can also be effective.

Plastic jig dressings suitable for jig trolling come in many different shapes, sizes, colors. Of all the plastic baits available, the twister tail continues to be one of the most popular and productive grubs.

Twister tails add color, bulk and action to the jig. All three features can increase the likelihood of the lure being spotted by nearby fish.

Let the water clarity be your guide when choosing grub bodies. In clear waters small two inch plastic bodies in natural colors work best. Smoke, grape, black or motor oil are good choices. In dingy water, larger three inch bodies and brighter colors get the nod. Fluorescent red, chartreuse, pink and orange are excellent choices in off color water.

A jig tipped with a plastic grub body can be fished clean or with live bait. In cool or cold water adding fish scent or using scented grub bodies is often an advantage. Fish seem to depend most on their sense of smell when the water is cool and their metabolism has slowed.

Jig trolling with live bait is a natural choice. Depending on the time of year, tip your jigs with a minnow, nightcrawler or leech. Minnows get the nod in the spring and fall when the water is cool. Crawlers and leeches are easier to keep alive and wiggling during the warmer summer months.

JIGGING ACTIONS & ROD SELECTION

Jig trolling is double deadly because it keeps four lines and lures in the strike zone at all times. Two primary jigging motions are the most productive and should be used interchangeably to determine which is best on any given day.

Sweeping the rod slightly forward then pausing the jigging stroke lifts the lure off bottom a few inches, and allows the bait to pendulum forward on a taunt line until it hits bottom. Maintaining a tauntness or slight tension in the line at all times helps the angler to detect light strikes. A passive jigging action, this technique moves the jig in a lift, pause, drop motion that is deadly on reluctant biters.

A second jigging action is more aggressive and requires the angler to pop the jig off bottom with a quick snap of the rod tip. The jig is then allowed to settle back to bottom on slack line.

Strikes that occur when the lure is swinging on a taunt line are easily detected as a tick in the line or a sensation of weight. Fish that strike the lure falling on slack line are a little more difficult to feel.

Both walleye and sauger are prime targets for jig trolling. A deadly structure fishing method, this sauger fell for a jig tipped with a crawler.

Most fish that hit a falling jig aren't detected until the angler starts his next jigging stroke.

Immediate hooksets are absolutely critical to angling success when jig trolling. Every second the angler delays his hookset reduces the odds of hooking the fish. An instantaneous and solid hookset are the best defense against short strikes and missed fish.

Stinger hooks are a logical step towards reducing missed or lost fish. Stinger hooks should be tied using No. 8 or 10 round bend treble hooks tied to eight pound test monofilament line. Using light mono helps to keep the minnow moving freely on the hook and leads to better catches.

Rod length is another way to make jig trolling more efficient. The angler controlling the boat uses longer rods to increase his or her horizontal lure coverage.

A medium action seven foot trigger stick makes a perfect rod for the angler controlling the boat. This rod features a fairly stiff action that helps to telegraph strikes, and is light enough to hold all day long. A quality baitcasting reel loaded with 8 pound test monofilament makes for a perfect jig trolling combination.

The second angler can get by nicely with medium action spinning rods. Again the rod should be fairly stiff to help detect light strikes and have enough backbone to offer head snapping hooksets. A graphite rod six foot or six foot, six inches long is ideal when matched with a lightweight spinning reel and premium six pound test line.

The monofilament line chosen for this angling system is also important. Selecting too heavy a line will make it difficult to maintain bottom contact. If the line is too light anglers will spend their valuable fishing time breaking off jigs.

An ideal jig trolling line should be limp, strong, thin and resistant to abrasion. Copolymer lines such as Stren's new Easy Cast or the time tested Magna Thin are perfect for jig trolling situations.

SUMMING IT UP

When all elements of the system are put together, jig trolling

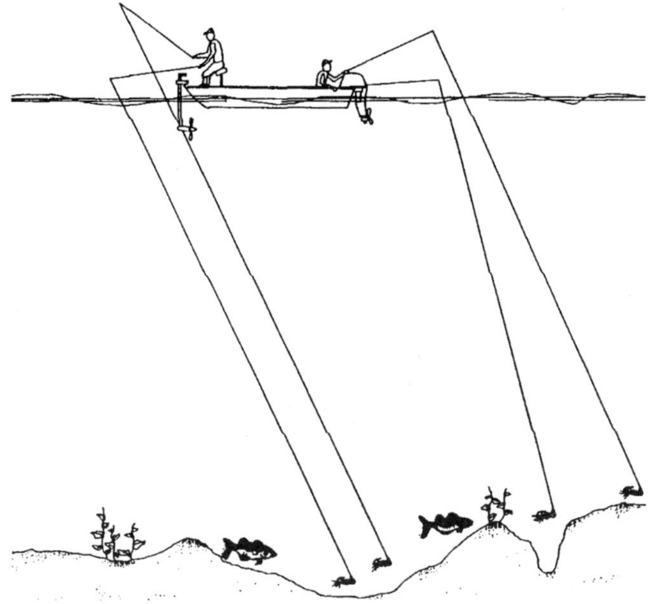

Jig trolling works best when two anglers work together as a team.

becomes a super efficient system for locating bottom orientated walleye. Among its best assets, this angling system can be used to fish a large amount of water in a short period of time. Jig trolling is also easily modified to allow for experimentation with lures, live baits, jig dressing and other presentation options.

Once a school of fish are located using this method, it's a simple step to slow down and fish the area more thoroughly or try other presentations. Once fish are located, slowing down and switching over to smaller jigs can turn a good fishing trip into one you'll never forget.

Combining jigs and trolling is a natural way to get more from what many anglers consider to be the most effective lure going. Simple and efficient, jig trolling systems are another way to tip the odds a little in the angler's favor.

In chapter five we'll focus on a little known walleye method; casting crankbaits. While crankbaits are an important part of the walleye fishing scene, few anglers understand the benefits of casting cranks.

Chapter 5

Casting Cranks

Walleye are aggressive predators. One look at that mouth full of sharp teeth says something about how walleye feed and what they prefer to eat. Meat. Specifically smelt, alewives, gizzard shad, emerald shiners, suckers, dace, drum, yellow perch and a wide range of other minnows and small fishes fall prey to the jaws of walleye.

When it comes to imitating the favorite food of the walleye, no lure does it better than a crankbait. Futhermore, with so many different brands, sizes, shapes and colors of these hard baits to choose from, walleye anglers have an endless supply of options to explore.

WHEN CASTING MAKES SENSE

Crankbaits casting is productive in many walleye angling situations. Whenever this popular species is found in shallow water (10 feet or less) a casting presentation deserves some consideration. Shallow water fish are spooky and can be difficult to approach. Casting allows anglers to cover water quickly while reaching out to nervous fish.

When walleye move into shallow water it's usually to feed. Shallow water walleye are actively hunting, aggressive and willing to strike at fast moving lures. Few lures can match the fish catching power of a crankbait when walleye are on the feed.

(Left) The author caught this walleye by casting a stickbait. Lightweight cranks require the use of a spinning combination and six pound test line.

A typical angler casting cranks can burn through water two or three times as fast as another common lure presentation like leadhead jigging. Crankbaits are also valuable tools for feeling out small pockets of cover (weeds or sunken timber) or bottom structure (rocks and breaklines) that consistently attract walleye.

With all this in mind, it's hard to imagine why casting crankbaits for walleye is rarely practiced.

WHERE TO CAST CRANKS

Knowing where to get started casting cranks is a big advantage. Many of the best places to cast cranks are spots overlooked by anglers in a hurry to get to the more popular areas.

Shorelines with a sharp lip, undercut or wash out area right up against the bank are excellent places to cast crankbaits. Anywhere a few feet of water meets the shore, walleye prowl the edges searching for baitfish they can trap against the bank.

When the wind blows into these areas baitfish are pushed towards shore where wave action muddies up the water. The cloudy water makes it difficult for baitfish to avoid prowling walleye that eagerly slurp up the confused and disorientated baitfish.

Some years ago while prefishing for a tournament I blundered into a shallow water walleye pattern that still leaves me smiling. The situation was a slow moving river. I broke off a jig on bottom and was tying on another one when I realized the boat was about to drift into shore.

As I used the electric motor to pull away from shore, I glanced at my sonar and noticed the water was actually deeper along the bank than the area I had been casting to. A little more investigating proved that the bank dropped off sharply into a narrow trench that paralleled the bank.

I lip hooked a minnow with the jig and flipped the offering right up tight to the bank. BANG! Almost immediately I was into a nice walleye. A second cast produced another fish but the third and forth casts snagged bottom and had to be broken off. The area was alive with walleye, but broken rock and wood on the bottom claimed jigs almost as fast as I could tie them on. In frustration I tied on a diving crankbait and casted the bait downstream. Using the electric motor to hold my position in the current, I retrieved the bait steadily until I felt it hit bottom then backed off and let the bait wobble against the current. Slowly I worked the bait forward.

When I was about to lift the lure for another cast a walleye jumped all over the bait! Casting and slowly retrieving a crankbait against the current turned out to be the ideal presentation. The slow moving crank was more than the walleye could stand and the problem with snags all but disappeared. The key was to slow up the retrieve the moment the bait could be felt hitting bottom and allow the lure to work in the current just off bottom. When the crankbait did occasionally hang-up, I simply gave the lure some slack line and the force of the current washed the bait free.

Shoreline points are also excellent areas to cast crankbaits. The best submerged points are those that stretch well out into the lake or reservoir and feature some rock rubble or scattered weeds on top of the structure.

If the point drops off sharply into deeper water, so much the better. Walleye are likely to be found right up on top early and late in the day or after dark. During the middle of the day, walleye often hold adjacent to the point along the first drop off or in slightly deeper water.

Weed edges that parallel the shoreline are another good bet for crankbait walleye. In many bodies of water these weed edges meander for miles, providing an almost endless supply of fishing opportunities. Typically the spots that attract walleye are cups, inside turns, points and other changes in the weed edge.

Broad leaf weeds like curly leaf cabbage are among the most attractive to walleye, but coontail, smart weed and other aquatic growth can also hold good numbers of fish.

A crankbait designed for bass fishing is among the best choice when fishing weeds. The legendary Rat-L-Trap is a lipless bait that slices through weeds much better than lures with a diving lip. I was pike fishing the day I discovered how deadly a lipless crank can be on walleye. I chose to work a weed edge where a flat covered with dense cabbage weeds suddenly dropped off into deep water. Cabbage weeds were scattered along the drop, thinning out in about 10 feet of water.

My plan was to work a lipless crank right along this edge in hopes of finding a trophy northern pike. What I found instead was a school of 18-24 inch walleye. I casted parallel to the weed edge and let the crank sink for approximately eight seconds before putting my rod tip in the water and beginning a moderately fast retrieve.

My first fish came right at the side of the boat, slashing at the bait as I lifted it from bottom. Expecting a pike, not a walleye I figured the fish was a fluke. In the next hour over a dozen walleye fell prey to the Rat-L-Trap. Since this first experience fishing walleye with lipless cranks, I've taken fish many times in similar situations.

I've learned that fishing cranks in weeds must be an aggressive presentation. When the bait catches on weed stems, snap the rod tip sharply. This snapping motion pops the bait free and often triggers explosive strikes from walleye that were giving chase.

Bays that feature emerging weed flats are also very attractive to walleye. Early in the season, these flats can be effectively cranked using shallow diving baits that skim over the top of the developing weed growth.

Back bays are at their best in early spring when the water is slightly warmer than the main lake body. Baitfish head for the warmer water where the plankton (food) level is higher and weed growth provides more cover from predators. These shallow bays often produce best early in the morning, late evening and after dark.

Wind swept reefs that top out in water six feet deep or less are excellent places to crank for walleye. The best reefs are those that drop into deep water with a series of stair step drop offs. This type of reef provide walleye a place to feed and rest with deep water security nearby.

The bigger the reef, the more rock, weeds and other cover available, the more walleye these spots attract. Reefs in remote areas are also likely to hold a few more fish as compared to those near popular

Casting cranks is an excellent alternative to casting jigs. Cranks can be worked through an area quickly when hunting for active fish.

fishing grounds. Fishing pressure can quickly turn a reef sour, especially if anglers cruise right up to the structure with their gasoline motor running.

Shallow water walleye are best approached with a silent electric motor.

When shoreline points extend into deep water, walleye will often suspend off the tip of the point. Casting diving cranks is an excellent way to tap into fish that are overlooked by structure fishermen.

When walleye suspend off the tip of points, they are most likely to strike crankbaits during the first hour of daylight, again in the evening and after dark. Low light levels provides the walleye a sight advantage over baitfish. That's why walleye often bite better when a wind churns up the water surface and reduces light penetration on cloudy days.

River flats are super areas to cast crankbaits. Walleye often spread out on river flats featuring water from three to eight feet deep. These flats will often feature small depressions or sunken logs that offer walleye the ideal ambush site.

Walleye lay in these areas waiting for the current to wash food into reach. When casting cranks in current a slightly deeper diving lure than would be used to reach bottom in still water is required. The force of the current pushing against the line reduces the diving depth of crankbaits.

HOW TO CHOOSE CRANKBAITS

The crankbaits that work best on walleye are normally the long thin minnow imitations or those that resemble the many species of shad. Long thin cranks including the Fred Arbogast Snooker, Storm ThunderStick Jr. Deep Diver, Rapala Minnow and Smithwick Rattlin' Rogue closely resemble important walleye forage species including emerald shiners, spottail shiners, smelt, alewives and young of the year perch.

Shad style lures like the Fred Arbogast Shadeaux (pronounced shadow) Storm Rattlin' Thin Fin, Rapala No. 5 and 7 Shad Rap and Bill Lewis Rattle Trap are effective lures in waters where gizzard or thread fin shad are abundant.

Because the lures casted for walleye are sometimes small and lightweight, spinning tackle is required to make long accurate casts.

A six-foot or six-foot, six-inch spinning rod/reel combination loaded with eight or 10 pound test monofilament is ideal for casting. Copolymer fishing lines like Stren's new Easy Cast are a good choice for casting cranks. These high tech lines are thin, abrasion resistant and they have none of the memory problems associated with other lines.

Ideally cranks used for walleye fishing should be equipped with sticky sharp treble hooks. Use a hook file to put a knife-like edge on all the hooks, not just the back treble hook. It will also be necessary to re-sharpen hooks during the day.

In some cases it may be wise to replace the treble hooks that come on crankbaits with one of the several brands of premium hooks available. The VMC Vanadium Cone Cut, Mustad Triple Grip and Heddon Excaliber are state-of-the-art hooks that are lightweight and amazingly sharp. Each of these hooks is designed to hook and hold better than round bend trebles.

Crankbait color is usually a minor concern. I strive to use natural colors with shad or perch patterns when fishing in clear water and brightly colored fluorescent patterns in turbid water.

THE RETRIEVE

Two basic retrieves are required when casting cranks for walleye. The first retrieve is a stop and go motion that allows the bait to pause momentarily before darting on. This stop and go motion is accomplished by stopping the retrieve and allowing the bait to slowly float up, hang suspended or sink slowly.

A walleye that is following a crankbait will often strike at the lure when it stops or slows down. Use a sweeping motion of the rod to speed up or slow down the lure and accomplish the desired action.

Short pumping strokes with the rod builds in a darting action that can be very effective. This retrieve method seems to work best with long thin minnow imitating baits such as the jerkbaits favored by bass anglers.

A slow and steady retrieve is another effective technique. For best results the bait must come into contact with the bottom, sunken debris, rocks, weeds and other cover. The bill of the bait should bump bottom, churning up a cloud of mud and rebounding off debris in the lure's path.

It's a good idea to pause the retrieve a few feet before the lure reaches the boat. Pausing the retrieve provides walleye an opportunity to strike before the bait is pulled out of reach.

PICKING APART STRUCTURE/COVER

It's critical when casting crankbaits to take a close look at the cover or structure to be fished. To avoid spooking fish, start by casting out the shallow areas first and then moving progressively deeper.

Using quality polarized fishing glasses helps the angler see submerged rocks, weed edges, sunken logs and other likely targets. The hottest fish will likely be right on top shallow structure or weed tops. Once a few boats show up on the scene, the fish will quickly spook and drop down a depth notch or two.

Select a bait that will contact bottom or weed tops and casting ahead of the boat work the shallows with a few casts then move the boat forward and continue. Once the shallow water has been covered, change to a deeper diving lure and work the next depth contour and so on until the structure is completely covered.

Covering several different depth ranges may require several different lures. You can also add weight to crankbaits to make them fish deeper. Adding a split shot or two a few feet in front of a lure can increase diving depth by several feet.

Recently Storm Lures introduced a new product known as SuspenDots and SuspenStrips. These unique products are pieces of thin lead with an adhesive backing that allows the strips or dots to be quickly attached to crankbaits. The strips and dots can be attached to the lure, stacked on top of another or removed in seconds.

The dots are lighter than the strips and designed to make subtle changes in lures or to transform a floating/diving lure into a neutrally buoyant lure. For best results the dots should be placed on the belly of the lure, so the natural action isn't thrown out of wack. The dots can be placed near the nose of the bait to yield a slightly nose down orientation in the water or near the tail for the opposite effect.

The SuspenStrips are slightly heavier and are best used on large or very buoyant baits. Two SuspenStrips under the lip of diving lures causes the bait to have a dramatic nose down orientation in the water. When the bait is cranked down to the bottom, it can be worked among rocks and other debris with the long lip touching bottom and the hooks held upright and slightly off bottom. Adding SuspenStrips to the lip of crankbaits works best with minnow or shad shaped lures that feature a large lip.

Crankbaits are yet another tool walleye anglers have at their disposal. The next time you reach for a jig casting outfit, ask yourself if a crankbait wouldn't be a better presentation.

In the next chapter we'll explore a method of crankbait trolling that has become known as precision trolling. This angling presentation one of the newest and most exciting ways to catch walleye.

Walleye often trap minnows in areas where the bank drops off sharply. These areas are especially productive when the wind is blowing into them and are a perfect place to cast crankbaits.

Chapter 6

Precision Trolling Crankbaits

All crankbait trollers have one thing in common. They need to know how deep their favorite lures dive. Depth control is everything when trolling crankbaits. It doesn't take a rocket scientist to figure out that crankbaits won't catch walleyes, or any other species unless the lures are presented close to waiting fish.

Little in the way of reliable information on lure diving depth was available until 1989 when Fresh Water Fishing Hall of Fame member Mike McClelland stunned the tackle world with his book Crankbaits "A guide to trolling and casting depths of over 200 crankbaits." McClelland's trolling data soon proved to be a bench mark for crankbait fishermen.

All of McClelland's trolling data was based on lures fished at or near their maximum diving depth. A trolling lead of 120 feet was chosen by McClelland. Reportedly this lead length delivered 90% of the maximum diving depth with lipped crankbaits.

McClelland's data is backed up with reams of graph paper that show conclusively how deep various lures will run when trolled on 120 feet of line. Although McClelland's data has been well received, the 98 cent question quickly became how deep

(Left) Dr. Steve Holt is co-author of Precision Trolling a book that has become a bible among serious trollers.

will these lures run if shorter or longer leads are run?

That question remained unanswered until a second book, Precision Trolling, researched and written by Dr. Steve Holt, Mark Romanack and Tom Irwin took McClelland's data and crankbait trolling another step forward. Precision Trolling was based on data collected by actually observing crankbaits trolled past a scuba diver.

Each lure was trolled past the diver with 15, 30, 60, 90, 120, 150, 180, 200, 220 and 250 feet of line out. The depth ranges achieved using these leads were recorded and later plotted onto a graph Holt refers to as a dive curve. The dive curve clearly shows the downward diving angle for each crankbait, making it possible to quickly and accurately determine the exact lure diving depth for any lead length from 15 to 250-feet.

Next the authors superimposed a life-sized picture of the lure onto a dive curve printed with easy to read "feet down" and "feet back" measurements. The life-size picture of the crankbait makes positive lure identification easy. Even if you don't know what brand or model of lure you're using, the bait can be quickly identified by comparing the lure photos on various dive curves.

The dive curves are printed on card stock and plastic laminated to make them waterproof. Connected together with a spiral binder, the booklet comes packaged in a reusable plastic clam pak that makes a handy place to store the book between fishing trips. Precision Trolling contains dive curves for 112 crankbaits including baits produced by Storm, Rapala, Rebel, Reef Runner, Bomber, Luhr Jensen, Cotton Cordell, Lindy Little Joe, Poe's and Bagley. In addition, dive curves are provided for Dipsy Divers, Jet Divers, lead core line and snap weights. Also included, approximately 40 pages of text provides detailed trolling tips.

Anglers who wish to order a book may do so by calling Crankbaits "In-Depth" Publications at 1-800-353-6958. The laminated version sells for $24.95 plus $4.00 shipping and handling. A paper version is also available for $19.95 plus shipping.

An auto-pilot is an excellent investment for those who spend a lot of time trolling. The TR-1 mounts on a small gasoline kicker motor and uses a simple hand-held remote control.

All the testing and dive curve data in Precision Trolling is based on 10 pound test monofilament. Those anglers who troll using lighter or heavier monofilament line can consult a handy line conversion chart provided in the book. There's also a line conversion chart for anglers who use super braid lines such as FireLine.

All lure testing was conducted with Daiwa SG27LC (line counter) reels to measure lead lengths. The most popular method of monitoring lead length, the SG27LC reels proved to be very accurate when filled to capacity with 10 pound test monofilament. The authors recommend selecting a durable trolling line like Stren Super Tough or High Impact. These lines feature the ideal properties needed in a trolling line, including low stretch, good knot strength, high abrasion resistance and consistency.

THE FACTORS OF LURE DEPTH

Monitoring trolling lead is a critical element of precision crankbait trolling. However lead length is only one of the factors that determine how deep a crankbait will dive. Line diameter, the amount of line out and the shape, lip size and buoyancy of the lure all combine to determine maximum diving depths.

The line diameter or pound test best for walleye and general trolling is an often debated topic. Ideally a line suited for walleye trolling must be small enough in diameter to allow lures to dive deeply, while being strong enough to handle fish safely.

According to the authors, 10 pound test is the ideal line for walleye trolling. "Lines smaller in diameter than 10 pound test are okay for trolling, but the thiner line has more stretch that leads to poor hooksets," comments Steve Holt. "Small diameter lines also abrade more easily and may potentially fail at the worst possible moment."

"Lines larger than 10 pound test significantly reduce lure diving depth," claims Holt. "A 1/4 ounce Storm Hot 'N Tot maxes out it's dive curve at 15 feet on 10 pound test line. The same lure and lead combination fished on 17 pound test line will only dive to about 11 feet."

The amount of line let out is a strong influence on how deep a crankbait will dive. McClelland's book states that crankbaits will reach 90% or more of their maximum diving depth when 120 feet of lead is used. The authors of Precision Trolling came to a different conclusion.

"Every crankbait is an individual that has its own distinctive diving curve," says Holt. "Some lures reach their maximum diving depth with 120 foot leads, but many lures, especially deep divers are just getting warmed up at 120 feet."

Holt, Romanack and Irwin experimented with longer lead lengths than tested by McClelland. "In some cases we saw lures continuing to dive even after letting out 260 feet of line," claims Holt. "The Luhr Jensen Powerdive Minnow is an excellent example. A lure with an extra large diving lip, the Powerdive achieved a depth of 25 feet with a 120 foot lead and 35 feet when trolled on a 260 foot lead."

"The Powerdive minnow picks up an additional 10 feet of diving depth when run on very long leads," adds Holt. "A significant depth improvement, this lure and other super deep divers are capable of reaching greater depths than we ever dreamed possible."

Ironically, not all big lipped lures turn out to be the deep divers they appear to be. The body size and buoyancy appears to have a major impact on how deep a lure will dive.

"The Rebel D-30 Spoonbill is a good example of a lure I expected to be a super deep diver," comments Holt. "After testing the Spoonbill D-30 and learning that it only dives to 18 feet, I was sure the lure tested had to be out of tune. After testing several other D-30 Spoonbills, I finally came to the conclusion that this bait which appears to be a deep diver is actually a medium depth diving lure.

TROLLING SPEED

It's a common misconception that trolling speed influences a crankbait's diving depth. It does not! Within the ranges of normal use, crankbaits will dive to the same depths regardless of trolling speed. The exception of course are lures that are out of tune and not running properly.

The authors of Precision Trolling discovered that lures trolled at 1 to 3 MPH all achieved the same maximum depth, but lures trolled slowly took a little longer for the baits to reach depth.

Trolling speed does however have a profound effect on lure action. Certain baits have little or no action at slow speeds and must be pulled at a brisk clip to be effective. Other baits simply can't be trolled fast or their subtle action is lost and the bait becomes worthless.

The best way to determine the ideal trolling speed for individual baits is to observe them running near the boat. Place the crankbait in the water and adjust the trolling speed until the lure responds with the best possible action. Make sure the bait is tuned properly and running straight through the water. If the lure wants to run left or right, the bait needs to be tuned by bending the line tie in the opposite direction the bait wanders.

Tuning crankbaits is a tricky business. It takes patience to determine the ideal action for each lure. Some lures run properly right out of the box. Others need a little fine tuning to get the most action.

Most crankbaits run best when attached to the line using a small fast lock snap. Make sure the snap used doesn't include a swivel and be sure the snap is rounded in shape so the lure has a free range of movement.

A polamar knot is the best way to attach a snap to monofilament fishing line. The strongest knot available and easy to tie, consult any package of fishing line for instructions on how to tie the polamar knot.

Line bow while trolling is another factor worth exploring. "I noticed during many dives that most of the monofilament on a long lead floats on the surface," commented Holt. "With diving crankbaits, only the last few feet of line angles down sharply to the lure. When trolling, a large bow of line forms between the rod tip and the lure."

Bow in the fishing line is a counter productive factor that makes it more difficult to hook fish while trolling. Before a fish that strikes a crankbait trolled on long leads can become hooked, the bow in the monofilament line must be pulled taunt.

"There's no doubt that walleyes routinely strike at passing crankbaits, but before the line pulls tight enough to set the hook they sense something is wrong and drop the bait," claims Holt. "No one knows for sure how much this phenomenon occurs, or how many fish are not hooked because of this fact of trolling."

There are several ways anglers can increase the odds of hooking the fish that bite. Trolling with the shortest leads possible helps to reduce the elapsed time between when a fish bites and the line pulls tight. Anglers can also try trolling a little faster than normal when the fish are biting well, but are not getting hooked up solidly. A faster trolling speed also reduces the amount of elapsed time between the strike and hookup and may also work to set the hook with more authority.

Thirdly, using lines with a minimum amount of stretch is an advantage when trolling crankbaits. Wet monofilament line stretches like a rubber band. The more you pull on it the more it stretches and the tougher it becomes to set a hook solidly. Certain types of monofilament are formulated for low stretch.

Trolling with slightly heavier lines may also help reduce line stretch problems. Trolling with 12 pound test line reduces lure diving depth by approximately 5%, while significantly reducing line stretch problems associated with eight pound test line.

"There's no perfect system that guarantees fish that bite a crankbait are going to get hooked and landed," admits Holt. "I put the odds in my favor by using the sharpest possible hooks. Thin wire round bend style treble hooks stick, penetrate and hold better than hooks made from tempered wire. Anglers may also elect to replace the treble hooks that come on their favorite crankbaits with premium quality hooks including the Mustad Triple Grip, Heddon Excalibur and VMC Cone Cut. These hooks are among the sharpest on the market and each is designed to

In-line boards such as the Off Shore Tackle Side-Planer are a invaluable crankbait trolling tool.

stick and hold better than traditional hooks."

For anglers who decide to replace the hooks on their crankbaits, it's wise to stay with the same size hook or in some cases one size larger can be used. If too large a hook is selected, the balance and action of the crankbait can be destroyed.

With Precision Trolling as a guide, crankbait trolling isn't such a mystery to the average angler. In fact, there are three easy steps to successful crankbait trolling.

The first step is to locate fish with the help of your electronics. On large bodies of water begin by selecting a manageable piece of water. It helps to image the water as a grid system of parallel lines. The boat moves along these imaginary lines searching for fish. If no fish are located, the boat moves over a few hundred yards and makes another pass until fish are located.

Unfortunately fish can't be effectively marked with most electronics if the boat is moving much above trolling speed. In order to speed up the process of locating fish, try running the boat at trolling speed for a few hundred yards while watching the graph closely, then speed up for few hundred yards. This scan and run method of hunting for walleye works equally well on open water or structure loving fish.

The second step requires the angler to select lures that will dive to the depths which correspond to fish marking on the graph. Select a variety of lure shapes, sizes and colors using the appropriate lead length that presents these lures at or slightly above the level fish have been located at. When you know how deep your lures are running, catching walleye on crankbaits becomes a simple process of changing lures and lead lengths until the fish communicate which pattern they want.

The final step is an important one that many anglers lose sight of. Once a productive lead length and lure combination are determined, it's critical to reproduce this combination exactly by changing other lines over to the same set up. Adding more lines with identical lures and lead lengths completes the pattern. When you've reached this point, it's all down hill. The hard part is over and it's time to reap the benefits of precision trolling.

The dive curve data prepared by Precision Trolling is must have information for the crankbait troller. With this invaluable data crankbaits can be aimed at fish like a hunter aims a bullet.

In the next chapter we'll look at the fine science of testing, tuning and tweeking crankbaits to achieve maximum action and success.

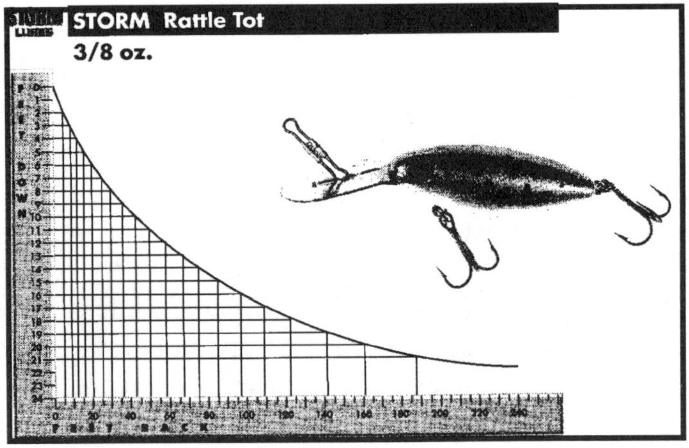

This dive curve of a 3/8 ounce Storm Rattle Tot is reproduced from the book Precision Trolling. When trolling crankbaits lead length and line diameter are the two factors that most influence diving depths.

Captain Ron Levitan trolls crankbaits from ice out to ice up with tremendous success.

Chapter 7

Tuning, Testing & Tweeking Cranks

Plugs, bodybaits, stickbaits, jerkbaits and a host of other more colorful names are used to describe what are known in angling circles as crankbaits. As a lure group, crankbaits have a reputation for being fickle. No other artificial lure requires the kind of routine adjustment, maintenance and down right patience to use as these minnow imitators.

Despite the fact that crankbaits often require a lot of tuning, tweeking and testing, these lures are amazingly productive. Among the best possible lure choice for those seeking trophy fish, crankbaits routinely produce larger than average fish.

Cranks also offer anglers an unlimited opportunity to add a personal touch to their lures. Painting, weighting, adjusting or otherwise fine tuning these lures into fish catching machines is half the fun.

TUNING

Making sure a crankbait is "in tune" or running true can not be over emphasized. The simple process of tuning can turn an ordinary crankbait into a fish killing machine. Think back to your own on-the-water experiences. How many times has a one particular lure out produced other similar baits? A crankbait that is

(Left) Crankbaits come in a wide variety of sizes, shapes and colors. In order to make these baits perform properly, they often need a little tuning, tweeking and testing.

even slightly out of tune won't produce as many fish as one that's tuned and working properly.

Lure manufacturers claim their baits are tuned and ready to run when you purchase them. In reality, many new crankbaits don't run properly out of the package. Crankbaits also go out of tune with use. A hooked fish thrashing in the net, accidentally stepping on a lure or slapping a lure on the water to free weeds from the hooks are common causes of lures getting out of tune.

Both new and used lures require periodic minor adjustments and in some cases major tune-ups to bring out the lure's fish catching ability.

A properly tuned crankbait should dive vertically into the water and run in a straight line. Lures can be checked for their tune by making a short cast and retrieving the lure with the rod tip pointed directly at the bait. You can also test the tune of a crankbait by trolling and letting approximately six feet of line out the back of the boat. If you check crankbaits while trolling, be sure to hold the rod a little to the side so the lure isn't running in the turbulence of the prop wash.

Also, keep in mind that certain lures aren't designed to run at high speeds. It may be necessary to slow down the retrieve or boat trolling speed when tuning certain lures.

Cranks often run slightly left or right of center causing the bait to tilt slightly on its side. To the unknowing eye these baits appear to be working fine. However, if the bait runs a little left or right it can't achieve it maximum diving depth and is more likely to "blow out" and come to the surface when retrieved at a fast pace or during turns. If two or more un-tuned lures are trolled next to one another they are likely to fowl each other causing tangle headaches. Furthermore, if a lure is out of tune it isn't giving off the vibration or action it was designed to provide.

Crankbaits usually feature an eyelet that comes straight out the nose of the lure, an eyelet that mounts in the diving lip or a wire connecting link. Lures such as the Storm Hot 'N Tot series that feature a wire connecting link can be tuned by bending it

The author is an avid crankbait fisherman. When properly tuned and used at the right times, crankbaits often produce larger fish than other lures and live bait rigs.

slightly with your fingers. Eyelets that are connected to the nose or lip of the lure must be bent with needle nose pliers. When tuning a crankbait, never bend the lip of the lure. If the lip gets bent, chances are the bait will be rendered un-tunable.

Adjust cranks that run to the left or right by slightly bending the line tie or eyelet in the opposite direction the lure is running. A trial and error process, bend the eye tie slightly and test the lure again. If a lure that was running left now runs right, you bent the line tie too far. Make small adjustments until the bait dives straight down into the water.

How a lure is attached to the fishing line can also make a difference in bait tuning. In most situations the best way to attach a crankbait to monofilament line is with a loop knot or a small Duolock style snap. These connection methods allow crankbaits to enjoy full freedom of movement.

Never use a snap swivel or ball bearing swivel when casting or trolling crankbaits. This extra hardware can influence the action of the lure and make tuning the bait more difficult.

If the lure features a split ring attached to the eyelet, the line may be tied direct to the split ring with any quality knot. If the lure features a small snap attached to an eyelet, tie directly to the snap. Never attach a snap on a line to a snap on a crankbait.

Certain lures such as shallow diving stickbaits usually feature a wire line tie that comes out the nose. If an angler ties a knot directly to the eyelet the lure action can be modified as desired by positioning the knot at the top, middle or bottom of the eyelet. When using this method, the knot must be repositioned as each fish is hooked and landed.

TWEEKING

Once a lure is tuned there are a number of modifications that can be done to change the lure's action, appearance in the water or function. Anglers have been trying to improve upon the natural fish catching action of crankbaits since the early days of sport fishing when these lures where hand carved from wood.

Drilling holes and filling them with weight is a common method used to change the action, running depth and orientation of a crankbait. For the record, anglers who drill holes in crankbaits usually end up with more discarded experiments than fish catching creations.

However, with a little care and patience floating lures can be weighted to suspend or sink in the water by carefully drilling holes and filling them with lead shot. Wooden baits such as the Fred Arbogast Snooker, Rapala Minnow or Bagley Bang-O-Lure are excellent candidates for drilling and adding weight. Depending on where the hole is drilled and the weight added, these lures can be made to have a nose down, level or nose up orientation in the water. Small BB sized lead shot are pressed into the hole and a dab of epoxy glue used to fill the hole.

Storm Lures offers a less labor intensive method of adding weight to a crankbait. A lead tape that can be stuck on crankbaits makes it easy to change the weight, balance and action of wood and plastic crankbaits. Known as SuspenDot and SuspenStrips, the dots are lighter and best suited to minor changes. The strips are slightly heavier and suitable for making major changes or working with very buoyant baits.

The best place to position these lead dots or strips is on the belly or lip of crankbaits. Placing a strip or two along the diving bill of a crankbait causes the lure to have a nose down orientation in the water. When fished in a darting motion near bottom these lures closely imitate foraging baitfish. The nose down orientation causes the bait to dive deeper and also positions the hooks up and away from potential snags.

A few dots positioned along the belly can turn a floating lure into a suspending or slowly sinking bait. Bass fishermen who fish jerkbaits have found this trick enables them to gain a little extra depth, slow down their presentation and fish in the face of bass living in heavy cover.

A quick and easy fix for lure adjustment, the Storm SuspenDots and SuspenStrips have become very popular. Cranks can also be weighted by wrapping lead wire around the treble hooks or by adding tiny sinkers to the split rings on the treble hooks. Both methods enable the angler to fish jerkbaits deeper and to change the action of these productive lures.

Simply adding a split shot a few feet ahead of the lure is another way to transform a floating bait into one that sinks. Anglers who troll at night for walleye often use a couple split shots to take their lures down deeper. Also, the shot stops debris that may slide down the line and fowl lures. This trick is especially useful in the summer when weeds are thick and in the fall when leaves floating in the water frequently catch on the line and foul trolled lures.

The tweeking of crankbaits doesn't stop with weighting tricks. Many anglers improve the hooking ability of their favorite lures by replacing the factory hooks with high performance after market trebles. Ultra sharp, ultra strong and ultra light treble hooks can transform an ordinary crankbait into one that sticks any fish that touches it.

Several hook manufactures offer treble hooks that offer improved sharpness and hooking ability. The Mustad Triple Grip, Heddon Excaliber, Owner Tournament Treble and VMC Vanadium are premium quality hooks that stick and hold better than ordinary trebles.

When replacing treble hooks select models that are the same size or one size larger than those equipped at the factory. Using treble hooks one size larger is a common trick among pro fishermen who demand maximum hooking and holding power from their lures. If too large a hook is used the action of the bait may be destroyed.

The hooking ability of most treble hook equipped lures can also be improved by bending the hook point out slightly with a pair or needle nose pliers. This trick works best with wire hooks that are easy to bend. Don't bend open the hook gap on premium quality hooks. Many of these hooks have been engineered with offset bends that hook and hold effectively.

Several crankbait manufacturers install premium hooks on

A sight like this is enough to make any walleye angler smile.

their most popular lures. Popular lures available with these high quality hooks include the Bomber series equipped with Heddon Excaliber rotating treble hooks, Fred Arbogast Mud Bug armed with Mustad Triple Grip hooks and Reef Runner Lures with VMC Vanadium hooks and many others.

Premium quality treble hooks are expensive; often costing a dollar a piece. Replacing all the treble hooks on a collection of crankbaits could run into money. Instead, most anglers replace the hooks on their favorite or most productive lures. Another option is to add one premium hook to each crankbait. When only one hook is replaced, change out the back hook and make sure the other hooks are sharpened to a razor edge.

Every hook on a crankbait should be honed to a sticky sharp edge. A file or stone is the age old way of sharpening hooks. Hone or file the hook on three sides to create a cutting style edge and a point free of burrs. A time consuming task, the effort put into sharpening hooks pays great dividends in landed fish. Even premium quality hooks may need a sharpening touch up after they have been used a little.

The finish on a crankbait can also be easily customized. Paints, die coats and flash tape are three easy ways to change the color or add flash to lures. It's best to purchase paints in small bottles. Hang cranks on a string over a layer of newspaper, paint as desired and let the baits hang overnight until dry.

Die coats apply like paint, but they dry quickly and the translucent colors allow base colors to show through. Most die coats dry in a matter of seconds and can be removed with a rag soaked in solvent. An excellent way to add color to the side or lip of a crankbait, these unique products are available in every color of the rainbow.

Adhesive backed flash tape is another quick way to add a touch of color or flash to a favorite lure. Available in sheets that can be cut with sissors or in pre-cut shapes, flash tape is available in countless colors and pattern choices.

Minnow imitating crankbaits do a wonderful job of fooling

fish right from the package, but many anglers can't resist adding their own personal touches to their favorite lures. A minor adjustment here, a little paint there and an ordinary crankbait can be transformed into a fish catching machine. The next time you reach for a crankbait remember that when these hard baits have been tuned and tweeked to perfection there's no limit to the fun they can provide.

Moving on to chapter eight, it's time to explore how weather (especially cold fronts) influences crankbait fishing techniques and success.

CHAPTER TIPS

1. A crankbait can't catch fish effectively if it isn't tuned properly. Check every crankbait to be sure it is running straight in the water before casting or trolling with it.

2. The best tool for tuning most crankbaits is a small pair of needle nose pliers that are used to bend the eye tie slightly left or right.

3. Never bend the lip of a crankbait. If the lip becomes bent, chances are the bait will be rendered untuneable.

4. When replacing the hooks on crankbaits use the same size or one size larger treble hook. If too large a hook is used the action of the lure may be destroyed.

5. Drilling holes in crankbaits and adding weight is risky business. If weight must be added to a crankbait it's best to use Storm's Suspend Strips or wrap lead wire around the hook shank.

Chapter 8

Trolling In Cold Fronts

It's the same old story. The fish are popping big time on half a dozen models of crankbaits, then Saturday rolls around and a nasty cold front blows into town. Anglers armed with day old bread for information find out quickly the cranks and colors that produced limits just a day or two ago are useless in these conditions.

It happens so often, if you didn't know better you might think there's a conspiracy going on. Alas, when a cold front hits town the fishing is going to be tougher, but the situation isn't hopeless.

Being "adaptable" is about the best advice one angler can give another when it comes to fishing for walleye in cold fronts. Whether it's fishing tournaments, running a charter boat or simply chasing walleye a few weekends a year, those anglers who are rigid in their fishing method are almost certain to struggle when the weather suddenly changes.

Cold fronts dramatically change fishing conditions. As a result fishing methods must change accordingly. When a front brings colder air, wind and rain you can bet on a few things happening. First, the fish are likely to move deeper. If the fish are suspended over open water they will simply drop down in the water col-

(Left) Bruce DeShano, owner of Off Shore Tackle, holds his popular Side-Planer board. Designed to troll fast or slow, in-line planers are a valuable tool for trolling in cold front conditions.

Subtle action crankbaits like this Jr. ThunderStick are among the best producers when trolling in tough cold front conditions.

umn. If the fish are using bottom structure, they will likely seek out slightly deeper water off the edges of the same structure.

Secondly, walleye effected by cold fronts tend to make brief feeding forays. When a bite occurs, it will probably only last a few minutes. There's a lot to be said for being in the right spot at the right time. During cold fronts it's not a bad idea to pound normally productive spots until the fish move up and turn on.

Thirdly, walleye are less likely to chase a meal when feeding in frontal conditions. Translated into language anglers can understand, that means SLOW DOWN YOUR TROLLING SPEED! Just as important, slow down the action on the lures selected.

During stable summer weather conditions, trolling with high action diving crankbaits such as the Storm Rattle Tot and Wiggle Wart, Bomber 7A & 8A, Cotton Cordell Wally Diver, Luhr Jensen Hot Lips and Reef Runner Deep Diver is almost a guarantee of fishing success. These lures have a fish hunting action that is ideal when trolling at high speeds making them ideal for covering water quickly.

In frontal conditions, high action cranks are the lures least likely to produce! Now's the time to switch to trolling presentations primarily used to catch walleye in April and November when the water temperature is between 40-50 degrees. High action diving baits are packed away and subtle action stickbaits including the Storm ThunderStick, Rapala Husky 13, Smithwick Rattlin' Rogue, Rebel Minnow, Cotton Cordell Ripplin' Red Fin, Bagley Bang-O-Lure and Bomber 15A are selected.

These shallow diving lures can be presented at any depth with the help of Off Shore Tackle's Snap Weight in-line sinker system. Simple and effective, Snap Weights are simply a lead sinker attached to a pinch pad model OR16 Off Shore Tackle release via a split ring. The release has a strong spring tension that holds the weight firmly on the line.

The angler puts the Snap Weight on the line anywhere between the lure and rod tip and removes the weight from the line when reeling in a hooked fish. Weights ranging from 1/2 ounce up to eight ounces, depending on water depth and trolling speed, can be fished using this system.

An ideal method of presenting subtle action/shallow diving crankbaits in deep water, Snap Weights have quickly gained in popularity among tournament and recreational anglers. The standard trolling method used with Snap Weights involves letting out a 50 foot lead, attaching a Snap Weight, then letting out an additional 50 foot of line. Dubbed the 50/50 system, this method works well with both spinners or diving crankbaits and has become the most popular Snap Weight fishing method.

In cold fronts, try modifying this system slightly by using a much shorter lead between the lure and the Snap Weight. Placing the Snap Weight six to 10 feet from to the lure makes it easier to control lure depth. Also, placing the Snap Weight close to the lure prevents crankbaits from floating up and out of the strike zone when the boat turns.

A more immediate action is imparted to cranks during turns and surges when short leads are used in combination with Snap Weights. The depths fished can be controlled by using various size trolling weights and by varying the lead length used.

In-line boards, such as the Off Shore Tackle Side-Planer are a great way to improve trolling coverage when fishing Snap Weights. On open water run two boards per side. When fishing smaller pieces of bottom real estate, try fishing a board on each side of the boat and a couple flat lines to round out the trolling coverage.

The ideal trolling speed when fishing Snap Weights in cold front conditions ranges from 1 to 1.5 MPH. Using a slower trolling speed keeps the lures in the strike zone longer and helps to tease strikes from walleye that are reluctant to strike fast moving forage.

When fish are located, make every effort to stay on the fish and make numerous passes through productive areas. Frontal conditions is no time to be sloppy about presentation. If you have a GPS or Loran-C unit save a waypoint for every fish caught and

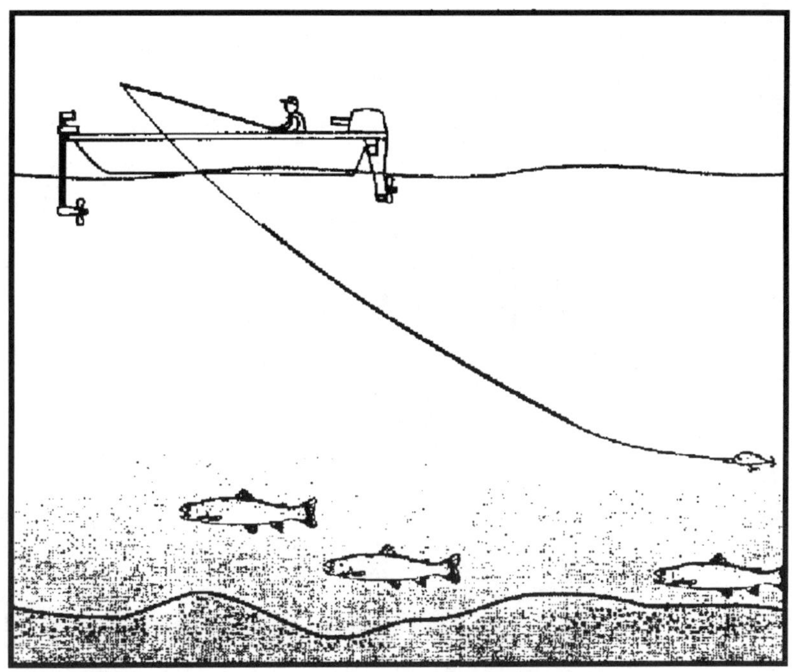

A typical segmented lead core set up using 90 feet of lead core and a 50 foot monofilament leader.

work these locations hard. If you don't have an electronic navigation system use a marker buoy, jug or shoreline sightings to stay on the fish.

Lead core line is another excellent method for trolling subtle action lures during cold front conditions. One of the best ways to fish lead core is to sandwich the lead trolling line between a monofilament leader and monofilament backing. Known as segmented lead core, this system usually consists of a 50 foot 10 pound test monofilament leader nail knotted to three colors (90 feet) of 18 pound lead core with 200 yards of monofilament backing completing the system.

There are no limits to the variations possible with segmented lead core. In shallow water situations it may only require one or two colors of lead core to get the job done. In deeper water more lead core can be used as needed.

When trolling lead core subtle action lures similar to those

Captain Al Lesh took this Saginaw Bay walleye with a deep diving subtle action crankkbait.

used with Snap Weights are attached to the leader. The leader and lead core line are let out slowly until the lure contacts fish or the bait strikes the bottom. In many cases all the leader and lead core are let out plus a considerable amount of monofilament backing. The more backing material that's let out the deeper the lead core will fish.

Long leads are the norm when trolling lead core. Not surprisingly this method is best suited to open water fishing where anglers can make long trolling passes.

Because lead core line is bulky, most anglers use large levelwind style reels for this fishing technique. Reels used for lead core fishing should be capable of handling at least 300 yards of 20 pound test.

Lead core is most often fished as a flat line. However, segmented lead core can also be fished in connection with in-line planer boards to increase trolling coverage.

When fishing lead core with boards the board must be attached to the monofilament backing. Many of the smaller in-line boards on the market simply aren't designed to handle the weight of lead core line. The Side-Planer produced by Off Shore Tackle is an excellent board for this type of fishing. A little larger than other in-line boards, the Side-Planer tracks to the side even when towing lead core and large crankbaits.

The next time a cold front threatens your fishing success, slow down, fish deeper, go to subtle action lures and use Snap Weights or lead core to reach the fish.

In chapter 9 the topic is trolling in rivers. When it comes to rivers most anglers reach for a jig. Here's how to make upstream trolling one of your most productive river fishing techniques.

Chapter 9

Trolling In Rivers

Jigging for river walleye is the kind of topic fishermen thrive on. Popular and productive, jigging is the traditional way to catch river run walleye. Trolling upstream with crankbaits instead of drifting downstream with jigs is an idea as foreign to most walleye fishermen as live bait is to bass anglers. Trolling in rivers breaks tradition and forces walleye anglers to rethink the way they fish flowing water.

In addition to being a breech of tradition, upstream trolling brings the often misunderstood crankbait into the picture. Few walleye anglers recognize crankbaits as deadly river walleye lures. In fact, many fishermen have yet to embrace the crankbait as a walleye producer.

WHY TROLL?

Considering the fact that jigging is productive most of the time, why troll upstream with crankbaits? Upstream trolling has some subtle advantages over most jigging presentations. First off, crankbaits are larger lures that make more noise in the water than jigs. Not surprisingly, crankbaits are easier for walleye to locate and catch in the murky river environment. The more the water becomes stained or off color, the more crankbaits excel and jig fishing suffers.

(Left) Dr. Steve took this 11 pound walleye by trolling a Storm Deep, Jr. ThunderStick upstream in the Kalamazoo River.

Secondly, upstream trolling allows the angler to control the speed of presentation much better than drifting downstream with the current. Using a small gasoline motor or an electric motor as a power source an angler can move upstream at a snails pace, at a brisk pace or any speed in between. The angler even has the option of hovering in one spot, allowing the wobbling crankbait to work its magic in the current, tempting walleye that may be reluctant to bite a bait quickly drifting downstream. In cold or muddy water, slowing down the presentation is critical to river fishing success.

Thirdly, upstream trolling assures that lures will be running in the strike zone 100% of the time. With most jigging presentations the lure passes in and out of the strike zone as the angler pumps the rod handle.

When upstream trolling the crankbait wiggles its way along within inches of bottom. If the lure fouls with weeds, leaves, small twigs or other debris, the vibration of the crankbait immediately stops tipping off the angler that the line needs to be checked and the bait cleaned of debris.

Snagged cranks are less of a problem than one might expect. So long as floating/diving style cranks are used, baits hung on bottom can be usually freed by simply giving the lure some slack line. The buoyancy of the lure and the rushing current work together to free most snags.

RIGGING OPTIONS

Upstream trollers have a couple rigging options to choose from. When fishing river flats and other areas where a slow to moderate current exists, floating/diving style crankbaits can be tied directly to monofilament and trolled behind the boat. This method works best in rivers that feature lots of water 10 feet deep or less.

A wide assortment of floating diving crankbaits can be used effectively for upstream walleye trolling. Anglers may be surprised to find that it takes a fairly deep diving lure to reach bottom in just six feet of water when trolling against the current.

The force of the current on the line and lure reduces the normal diving depth of crankbaits substantially.

The most popular choices are those baits that normally dive from 10-20 feet when trolled in still water. A few of the baits that consistently produce river walleye include the Fred Arbogast Mud Bug, Rebel Wee R series, Cotton Cordell Wally Diver & CC Shad, Storm Wiggle Wart & 1/4 ounce Hot N' Tot, Bomber 6A, Luhr Jensen 1/4 ounce Hot Lips and Rapala No. 7 Shad Rap.

For best results these baits must be equipped with sticky sharp hooks. Many of these lures are equipped with premium quality treble hooks. The Fred Arbogast Mud Bug features Mustad's new Triple Grip hooks and the Bomber 6A and Cordell Wally Diver signature series baits are equipped with Heddon Excalibur hooks.

In areas where the current is swift or the water deep, diving style crankbaits simply can't reach the bottom. A simple three way rig armed with a shallow diving crankbait is the answer in fast and deep water.

A 12-inch dropper is used with a lead weight heavy enough to easily feel bottom. The monofilament used to tie the dropper should be at least one break strength lighter than the main line. If the sinker becomes snagged, the angler can break it off without losing the leader and the valuable crankbait.

The leader on the three way rig should be three to five feet long. Shallow diving minnow baits are the best cranks for use with this rig. Excellent suggestions include the Fred Arbogast Snooker, Rapala No. 13 Floating Minnow, Storm Jr. ThunderStick, Bomber Long A and Smithwick Rattlin' Rogue. Fat bodied shallow divers may also be used in connection with a three way rig. The Luhr Jensen Speed Trap, Normark Shallow Shad Rap, Storm Thin Fin, Mann's 1 Minus and Bomber 2A are good choices.

When trolling on straight monofilament or using three way rigs, it's important to use thin diameter line. Line diameter has a dramatic effect on lure depth when trolling in river current. Extra thin diameter lines such as Stren's Magna Thin provide crankbaits greater depth diving range and make it possible to use lighter weights and still maintain bottom contact when fishing with three way rigs. Select line sizes ranging from six to 10 pound test for best results.

Three way rigging is also a good place to experiment with the new superbraid lines. Super thin in diameter and strong, these high tech lines are ideally suited to upstream trolling situations.

Anglers should fish superbraid lines cautiously. If a lure becomes snagged on bottom and the drag doesn't slip a broken rod may result. A light drag setting and soft action rods are a must when fishing with superbraid lines.

METHODOLOGY

River flats often attract scattered schools of feeding walleye. Upstream trolling with cranks is one of the fastest and most efficient ways of covering this water. A small gasoline motor is a workhorse for this kind of fishing, but a powerful electric motor may also be used if the current isn't too strong.

Depending on the size of the area to be fished, it may require several passes to completely cover all the places walleye may be hiding. Select a floating/diving style crankbait that will easily reach bottom when trolled 20-50 feet behind the boat. Let out line until you can feel the bait ticking bottom. Too long a lead will cause the lure to simply scour into the sand and bottom debris.

Long rods are an advantage when trolling in rivers because they allow the baits to reach out away from the boat and cover a little more water. An eight or nine foot steelhead spinning outfit makes a good upstream trolling rod. Also, seven foot triggersticks or eight foot backbouncing rods work well if the angler prefers baitcasting equipment.

In-line planer boards such as the Side-Planer produced by Off Shore Tackle are also handy for spreading out lines and covering water more throughly. When using in-line boards it's best if these mini skis are set to run 20-30 feet from the boat. Keeping the boards fairly close to the boat makes it easier to control where the lures are running, reducing the chances of snags or conflicts

These anglers are teaming up to remove an in-line board while trolling in the lower Detroit River. Boards are an easy and effective way to increase trolling coverage.

with other fishermen.

Vary the trolling speed depending on conditions. In cold or murky waters a trolling speed that barely makes headway against the current is best. Once the water warms to near 50 degrees, a faster trolling speed may trigger reactionary strikes from actively feeding fish. A faster trolling speed also has the advantage of allowing the angler to cover water quickly.

In high water conditions, walleye often feed very close to the bank. Areas to look for include spots where three to six feet of water can be located tight against the bank. Walleye herd minnows into these areas where they pin them against the shoreline, blocking their escape.

Slight depressions in the bottom will also hold walleye feeding on the flats. A depression in the bottom will show up readily on a quality liquid crystal graph. While the walleye using these spots may be belly to bottom and tough to mark on the graph, fish these areas throughly and make a mental note of their location for future trips.

Sunken logs, rocks and other debris in the water are also good places to find river walleye waiting for their next meal.

When a fish strikes, set the hook with a sharp rod sweep and immediately put the boat in neutral. Fight the fish as the boat slowly drifts downstream, watching that the boat doesn't drift into debris. Once the fish is landed, the boat is in position to make another pass through the same area.

When fishing with boards it's best to keep the boat moving upstream until the board is reeled in and removed from the line. Once the board is removed, put the boat in neutral and fight the fish as if it were hooked on a flat line.

River areas that feature a strong current or deep water such as the Detroit River are best fished with a three way rig and shallow diving crankbait. Three way rigs, often referred to as a Wolf River rigs are most effective when fishing deep river holes, long deep runs and riffles or other fast moving current areas.

The rig itself should be equipped with a lead weight that's heavy enough to make it easy to maintain contact with bottom. The angler doesn't drag the weight along bottom, but rather uses the weight to touch bottom every few feet while trolling. This touch-and-go fishing style insures that the trailing crankbait is positioned close to the bottom but above debris and other snags.

Depending on the water depth, trolling speed and depth of the water, the sinkers required for three way rigging may vary from 1/4 ounce to three ounces or more. When small weights are used a medium action spinning outfit makes a great rod for three way trolling. If heavier weights must be used to maintain contact with the bottom, stout medium or medium/heavy action baitcasting tackle is recommended.

Three way rigs may be trolled using a small gasoline motor or a powerful electric motor. In shallow water, a silent electric motor may be required to prevent spooking walleye with motor noise. Small aluminum boats can get by nicely with a 12 volt electric motor that generates 35-40 pounds of thrust. Larger boats may require the extra thrust and battery life of a 24 volt system. The new 36 volt electric trolling motors like MotorGuide's Beast provide up to 65 pounds of thrust by tapping into extra power provided by the cranking battery in your boat.

When upstream trolling with an electric motor, bow mounted units are recommended over a transom mounted electric. It's easier to control the boat by dragging it upstream with the help of a bow mounted motor than by pushing it upstream with a transom mounted unit.

In many cases it will be necessary to use a small gasoline motor to power the boat upstream. Kicker motors are the most efficient way to troll upstream against strong current.

When using a kicker motor, the angler must keep one hand glued to the control handle at all times to keep the boat on course. When both hands are needed to tie on lures or other tasks, put the motor in neutral and drift downstream with the current until ready to fish again.

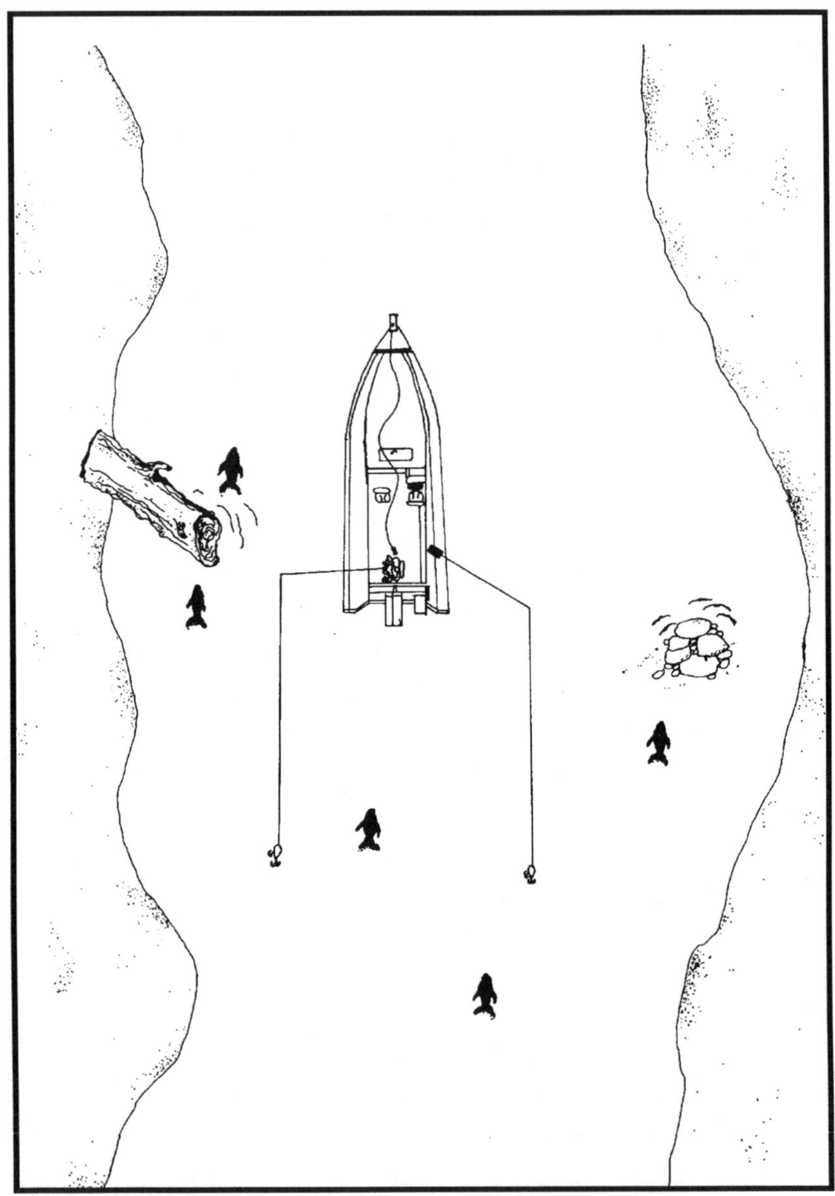

When trolling in rivers use two rods whenever possible. It usually works best to hold one rod while keeping a second line working from a handy rod holder.

Upstream trolling with three way rigs or diving style crankbaits provides anglers with a new twist on river fishing. Jigs may be the most popular river fishing lures, but crankbaits also have their place in rivers. This season break with tradition and see for yourself how effective trolling against the grain can be.

In the next chapter we'll discuss tactics for trolling up fall walleye using crankbaits. The rewards of this unique presentation are trophy walleye and lots of them.

CHAPTER TIPS

1. When trolling in current crankbaits don't dive as deeply as you might expect. To make up for the reduction in lure diving depth, use lures with a large diving lip or let out longer trolling leads.

2. Long rods such as those used by steelhead fishermen make excellent river trolling rods. The longer rods reach out away from the boat and help to present lures outside the noisy prop wash.

3. Brightly colored crankbaits usually work best in the off color waters of rivers. Also, baits with rattles are excellent choices for fishing in murky river water.

4. When a fish is hooked trolling upstream, put the motor in neutral to fight the fish. Fighting the fish while continuing to troll against the current puts too much pressure on the line and can lead to break offs.

5. Keep a log book of spots that produce while upstream trolling. These same areas are likely to hold fish time and time again.

6. A small rubber band half hitched over the line a few feet in front of the crankbait often helps to keep leaves and other debris from sliding down the line and fouling the crankbait.

Chapter 10

Trolling Crankbaits In The Fall

Fish won't bite on crankbaits in cold water. It's a statement I've heard countless times and one that brings a smirk to my face when some well meaning fisherman offers up this free advice. You know what they say about free advice? If free advice is worth what you pay for it, don't put away your crankbaits just yet.

Admittedly, a bit of truth survives in most fishing myths. Crankbait fishing for cold water walleye is no exception. Many anglers who have tried to troll up late season walleye struggle to catch fish. In fact, the fishing can be down right tough if summer time trolling techniques are used in cold water conditions.

The secret to cold water cranking is accepting the transformation that takes place from warm water trolling techniques to methods more suited to cranking in ice cold water. The adjustment isn't monumental, but one that requires the angler to use some special equipment, common sense and a willingness to catch the largest walleye in the lake!

UNDERSTANDING COLD WATER WALLEYE

The system begins by understanding what happens to walleye when the surface water temperature drops to 45 degrees or colder. The cooling water triggers an inborn urge to feed among

(Left) The best time to catch monster walleye like this one, taken by Gary Parsons, is during the late fall.

Trolling slowly, using subtle action crankbaits and in-line planer boards is the formula for all trolling success. These anglers are teaming up to land a Little Bay de Noc walleye.

walleye. Instinctively these fish know that winter and lean times are ahead. Feeding heavily during the fall period helps put on fat reserves that will be desperately needed months down the road.

During the fall, walleye feed actively and frequently. Unfortunately, walleye also become more selective in the size and type of forage they're interested in.

Big meals are what these toothy fish are after. Small minnows simply aren't worth the energy it requires to chase them. Even smallish walleye prefer a mouthful when feeding in cold water.

In addition to keying on larger sized forage, walleye prefer to feed on soft rayed fishes that are protein rich and easily digested. Fishes including whitefish, ciscoes, suckers, emerald shiners, gizzard shad, spottail shiners and smelt become the preferred forage of walleye during cold water periods. If these soft rayed species aren't present, the common yellow perch is a suitable alternative.

Most of these forage fishes have something in common. During the fall they are usually located in the deep water basins of the lake. Mud flats covered by 25-50 foot of water are prime places to seek out schools of these important baitfish.

Not surprisingly, walleye follow these wandering schools of bait into the deep water basins where they feed almost completely undisturbed by fishing pressure until ice up.

MATCHING THE HATCH

The term matching the hatch is one trout fishermen use to describe the type and size insect fish are feeding on. The same methodology applies to fall walleye trolling.

Anglers must select their crankbaits keeping in mind that the bait should look as much like the available forage as possible. In most walleye waters that means that baits with a long slender profile usually out produce short fat body lures.

Also, baits that float at rest and dive when pulled tend to be the best choices. It's tough to control the trolling depth of sinking lures. Sinking lures are speed dependant, meaning that the lures run deeper at slow speeds and shallower at faster speeds.

Baits that meet this floating/diving criteria are available in shallow, medium and deep diving models. Examples of excellent shallow diving baits include the Fred Arbogast 833 Snooker, Rapala Husky Jerk, Rebel F40S Minnow, Storm Jointed ThunderStick, Smithwick Suspending Rattlin' Rogue and Mann's Loudmouth.

Medium diving favorites include the Arbogast Snooker, Storm Jr. Deep ThunderStick, Mann's Stretch 10 & 15, Rebel D30S Spoonbill, Luhr Jensen 1/2 ounce Power Dive, Bomber 24A and Bagley Deep Bang-O-Lure.

Productive deep diving cranks with a long thin profile include the Storm Deep ThunderStick, Luhr Jensen 3/4 ounce Power Dive Minnow, Bomber 25A and Mann's Stretch 20 baits.

Lure color can also be a factor in matching the hatch. If perch are an important forage, baits that feature a perch or firetiger pattern are best.

Where shad, suckers, smelt or shiners are common the classic black back/silver side or Tennessee shad colors are good bets. Other colors that produce well in slightly stained waters include the metallic rainbow, metallic perch and gold/black back.

THE IMPORTANCE OF LURE ACTION

Every model of crankbait has a different action. In fact, even among identical model lures, some subtle differences in lure action occur.

The wiggles and wobbles these lures produce are their signature and one of the ways that walleye key in on a bait. Even subtle differences in lure action that we as anglers can't discern seemingly make a difference to the walleye.

That's why certain individual lures become hot, while others of the same or similar model go untouched. As anglers we've all seen it happen; one particular lure pounds fish while others survive without a scratch.

There's little an angler can do to duplicate the action of a bait that's working, besides trying other similar lures. As mentioned before, sometimes the differences in lure action are undetectable.

However, one of the most common reasons why crankbaits don't catch fish is because the bait is out of tune. For a crankbait to function properly it must pull straight through the water without turning on its side or veering left or right. Most crankbaits can be manually tuned by simply bending the line tie a little left or right. For a detailed description on how to tune crankbaits consult chapter 4 Tuning, Testing and Tweeking Crankbaits.

Generally speaking lures that feature a subtle top-to-bottom roll are better cold water producers than baits with a pronounced head-to-tail wobble. You can tell if a bait features a roll type action by watching the bait carefully as it moves through the water. If the top and bottom of the bait appears and disappears as the bait moves in the water it has a defined roll to it.

TROLLING SPEED

No magic formulas needed here. Slow, slower and slowest are the ideal trolling speeds for cold water walleye cranking. Common sense dictates that in cold water walleye are less apt to chase a fast moving lure. Trolling speeds typically range from .5 to 1.5 MPH. The colder the water becomes the slower anglers must fish to trigger strikes.

Trolling this slow requires some special equipment that many anglers may not have. A small gasoline kicker motor is essential for serious cold water cranking. Motors ranging in size from 6-15 horse power are ideal. Some 20 and 25 HP models may idle down slow enough, but larger motors aren't likely to produce these super slow fishing speeds.

A kicker motor is so essential to this and other walleye trolling techniques that not a single touring professional on the Pro Walleye Tour or North American Walleye Association circuits fishes without a kicker motor! That's a strong endorsement for the use of small gasoline motors.

GETTING DOWN AND DIRTY

Walleye may suspend in cold water, but these fish are more likely to be suspending near the bottom than the surface as is commonly true during the warm water season. Many of the crankbaits mentioned earlier are capable of diving 20-35 feet on their own. Unfortunately, more than one third of the long slender profile baits these fish are looking for are shallow or medium diving baits that run from eight to 15 feet.

Several angling methods are used to take these diving lures to greater depths. One of the more effective deep water trolling techniques has been around for generations.

Using lead core line is an excellent method of reaching maximum depths with shallow diving lures. Lead core line features a soft lead wire covered with a tough dacron outer coating. These lines come in pound test ratings like monofilament. Larger sizes of lead core line feature heavier lead wire that can more easily reach greater depths.

For walleye trolling applications most anglers select 18 or 27 pound lead core line. Most lead core lines are color coded to help the angler determine accurate lead lengths. A popular rigging method consists of three colors or approximately 90 feet of lead core line sandwiched between 200 yards of 10-12 pound test monofilament backing and a 30-50 foot monofilament leader.

Known as segmented lead core, this system is deadly when combined with floating/diving style crankbaits. The crankbait is attached to the leader using a snap, then progressive amounts of leader and lead core are let out and trolled behind the boat. Shallow, medium or deep diving lures may be used in combination with lead core line. For maximum lure depth, all the lead core line is let out plus progressive amounts of monofilament backing to increase lure depth as needed.

Depending on the lure and trolling speed used, lead core line can be used to reach fish 25-50 feet below the surface with ease. Lead core lines are most often fished as flat lines behind the boat, but they can also be fished in combination with in-line planer boards. The planer boards are attached to the monofilament backing and used to increase trolling coverage. The Off Shore Tackle Side-Planer is the largest in-line board on the market and best able to handle the drag of lead core line and deep diving crankbaits.

The biggest drawback to lead core line trolling are the super long leads needed to reach deep water fish. Leads that often exceed 250 feet are needed to achieve maximum lure depth with shallow diving lures.

Fishing with unique trolling sinkers known as Snap Weights is another method that's gaining in popularity among walleye fishermen. A Snap Weight is simply a lead sinker attached to a pinch pad type line release. The spring tension in the release is strong to hold the weight in place on the line until the angler removes it during the fight.

The use of Snap Weights is outlined in Chapter 3 Cold Front Crankin'. The trolling tactics provided in Cold Front Crankin' applies equally well to fishing during the cool water periods of the fall and spring. In fact, this unique trolling method is so deadly it warrants repeating.

The beauty of Snap Weights is they can be attached anywhere on the line, helping the angler separate his lures from the lead weights. A common rigging method used with Snap Weights requires the angler to let out a favorite crankbait 50 feet behind the boat, then attach a Snap Weight to the line and let out an additional 50 feet of line. This rigging is known as the 50/50 method and can be fished as a flat line or used in combination with an in-line planer board.

By using progressively larger sized sinkers, more depth can easily be achieved. Up to three ounces of weight can be used when trolling with Off Shore Tackle Side-Planer in-line boards and up to 12 ounces when fishing flat lines.

Both lead core and Snap Weight trolling are less than exact sciences. Because weight is used to achieve lure depth, these trolling techniques become speed dependant. The book Precision Trolling is an excellent guide to fishing lead core line and Snap Weights. The approximate lure running depths are provided on an easy to read chart that's based on trolling speed, lead length and the amount of weight attached to the line. This useful book also provides accurate dive curves for over 120 shallow, medium and deep diving crankbaits. Copies are available for $19.95 plus $4 shipping by calling Crankbaits "In-Depth" Publications at 1-800-353-6958.

A third trolling method sees little use among walleye anglers. A set of downriggers still rates as the best trolling depth control device.

For most walleye fishing applications a set of manual riggers is ideal. Small boat owners can benefit from portable models designed to clamp onto the gunwale of small aluminum boats.

A pair of downrigger weights and some dependable line releases complete the necessary hardware. Cannon balls ranging from three to six pounds are ideal for slow trolling speeds. These lighter weights create less water displacement that may spook fish when trolling. Spring tension pinch pad style releases like

In-line boards such as the Off Shore Tackle Side-Planer can be used with lead core line, snap weights and deep diving crankbaits.

those produced by Off Shore Tackle are among the most dependable available.

Trolling with downriggers has many advantages, the most obvious and beneficial of which is precise depth control. Used in combination with floating/diving crankbaits anglers can target fish marked at specific depths with great success.

Downrigger trolling also allows shorter trolling leads to be used, making it easier for the boat to be quickly turned around for another pass when a pod of fish are located. Most late season downrigger trollers favor shallow diving stickbaits that dive a few feet below the canon ball.

The late season trolling bite produces some of the biggest walleye taken every year. To those that aren't tuned into the specifics that make this trolling system work, the catches provided may seem more like magic than fishing skill.

Cold water cranking can be boiled down to a simple formula. Troll slow, fish large crankbaits with a minnow profile and concentrate on the deep water mud basins. Follow these simple steps and the late season may quickly become your favorite fishing season.

In the next section we'll explore live bait rigging in its many forms.

CHAPTER TIPS

1. Minnow shaped crankbaits with a subtle action are usually the best producing baits during the fall period.

2. The three best speeds for trolling during the fall are slow, slower and slowest. Keep trolling speeds below 1.5 MPH for best results.

3. Fall is when most of the trophy class fish are taken. Be sure to take along a camera to record those fish you don't plan on getting mounted.

Chapter 11

Slip Sinker Rigging

The term Lindy Rigging is as much a part of walleye fishing as slam dunking is to basketball. The Lindy Rig is a brand name slip sinker rig and along with about a dozen other similar products has over the years become one of the basic methods of catching walleye. Mastering the basics is the first step towards success in any persuit. When the subject is walleye fishing, live bait rigging is as basic as bread and water.

Designed to catch structure orientated walleyes, bottom rigging shines best when walleye are reluctant to bite other presentations such as jigging, casting or trolling. These methods are most productive when walleye are active and willing to chase a bait. When fishing gets tough, wise anglers reach for their slip sinker rigs, slow down their presentation and concentrate on teasing walleye into biting.

Slip sinker rigging has been described many ways. A fishing method that's been a part of walleye fishing for over three decades, rigging is simply a means of fishing that allows walleye to take the bait without feeling the weight. As simple to use as they are deadly, slip sinker rigs and walleye fishing are two topics that will forever overlap.

(Left) Slip sinker rigging is one of the slowest paced presentations used for walleye fishing. This live bait technique gets the nod when walleye won't hit lures that are dragged, casted or trolled.

The common slip sinker rig consists of a walking style sinker, a small swivel or snap, a short monofilament leader and a hook of some sort. The hooks used with slip sinker rigs vary depending on the type of bait used. When minnows are the bait a thin wire Aberdeen style hook is an excellent choice. Thin wire hooks penetrate with very little pressure, making them an excellent choice for live bait rigging.

Another excellent hook for slip sinker rigging is the Finesse hook produced by Mustad. This thin wire hook is similar to the Aberdeen except it features a slightly shorter shank and a turned up eye that makes it easy to snell. When fishing minnows a No. 1 or 2 hook works best.

If leeches are the bait a very light weight hook like the Mustad Finesse in a No. 4 size is ideal. This lightweight hook allows the leech to enjoy freedom to swim naturally. Using heavier hooks can prevent leeches from providing maximum swimming action.

Crawlers are often fished using a two hook snell tied using a No. 4 beak style hook. Similar to salmon egg hooks the beak hook features a turned up eye for snelling and is compact making it easy to hide in a crawler. Using a two hook harness helps to reduce short strikes so common when fishing with crawlers.

Floating jigheads and soft body floating jigs are also popular slip sinker rigging hooks. These hook/lures help to position the bait up off bottom and add a bit of fish attracting color.

Over the years the basic concept of slip sinker rigging hasn't changed much. The slip sinker weight positions the bait near bottom, meanwhile the bait gets slowly dragged along in a tantalizing manner. When the angler feels the strike, slack line is immediately fed to the fish, enabling it to eat the bait without feeling the weight of the sinker or pressure from the angler. If all works according to plan the walleye doesn't feel a thing until the angler reels up the slack line and sets the hook with authority.

Slip sinker rigging is a simple technique that's tough to improve upon. In some respects the original Lindy Rig is as successful today as it was 30 years ago. However, as with so many

The slip sinker rig is one of the oldest and most trusted of all walleye fishing presentations.

other aspects of fishing, this classic bottom rigging technique has been made more user friendly.

Northland Tackle provided one of the most important advancements in rigging when they introduced the Roach Rig. Designed and endorsed by Gary Roach (Mr. Walleye himself), the Roach Rig enables an angler to quickly adjust leader length without the time consuming process of cutting and tying new leaders.

A moveable sinker stop slides up and down the line with a little thumb pressure, allowing the angler to adjust leader length in seconds. In stained or off color waters, a short 24 inch leader is adequate. However, in clear water where walleyes are often spooky, a 36 to 60-inch snell is best. In extreme cases leaders up to 10 feet long are used. These long leaders are the exception rather than the rule.

The ability to easily adjust leader length is more incentive for anglers to experiment with this overlooked variable. An important aspect of rigging, leader length determines in part how far off bottom the bait rides, the action of live baits and in many cases the success or failure of this common fishing presentation.

When changing leader lengths, the rule of thumb is to start with a fairly short leader and go longer as conditions warrant. For all practical purposes, leader length should not exceed rod length.

The next logical step in the evolution of bottom rigs was to develop a convenient means of changing weights while fishing. When Quick Change Systems, a small company based in Pierre, South Dakota introduced their Sinker Clevice another break through in bottom rigging began.

A plastic device that threads on the line and accepts walking style sinkers via a small clip, the Quick Change Sinker Clevice enables anglers to change sinker weights without a second thought. Depending on fishing conditions, anglers can choose from 1/8, 1/4, 3/8, 1/2, 3/4 or one ounce rigging sinkers.

Changing weights enables the angler to effectively move from shallow to deep water or speed up the presentation while maintaining contact with bottom. A few of the Quick Change Sinker Clevices and some walking style sinkers in the common sizes are all the angler needs to get started using the Quick Change bottom rigging system.

The same Quick Change Sinker Clevice can be used to fish single arm bottom bouncers in snag filled waters. Rigging this way combines the virtues of a slip sinker and bottom bouncer into one walleye rig.

In place of a walking sinker, attach a single arm bottom bouncer to the sinker clevice. The bottom bouncer keeps the bait up off bottom and makes the rig more snag resistant. The ideal rigging method when fishing spinners, spin-n-glows and or other fast paced attractors, this simple set up enables the angler to feel the bite and feed the fish line if desired.

Another advancement in bottom rigging has been popular with steelhead and stream trout fishermen for years. Only recently have walleye anglers discovered the Slinky Drifter bottom rigging system.

More snag resistant than split shots, walking style sinkers

and other bottom weights, the Slinky Drifter consists of a flexible length of nylon parachute cord filled with various sizes of lead shot. A special tool is used to hold open the parachute cord while lead balls are inserted. Once the correct amount of shot is stuffed into the hollow cord, a match or cigarette lighter is used to melt and seal the ends of the cord.

Once the ends of the weight are heat sealed, the wire end of a small snap swivel is pushed through one end of the woven parachute cord material and pinched shut. Now this unique bottom weight is ready to be rigged like a traditional slip sinker rig.

Simply thread the line from the rod through the swivel and add a small plastic bead. Next, tie on a small barrel swivel. Various length leaders can be attached to the opposite end of the barrel swivel and a wide variety of baits and attractors used to fool walleye.

This effective bottom rig can be backtrolled, drifted or casted to walleyes found in snag filled real estate. The flexible nature of the Slinky allows the weight to slide along the bottom and over obstructions that would eat up walking sinkers and split shots.

The Slinky Drifter shines best in rocky environments, but this rigging system is equally at home in weeds or flooded timber. When fishing heavy cover, it's a good idea to use a weed-less style single hook such as the Eagle Claw 249W. This wide shank hook features a thin wire weed-guard that helps prevent the hook from fouling on weeds, wood and other debris.

Slinky Drifters can be purchased pre-made and ready to fish in popular weights or the components purchased separately and custom sinkers built for specific needs. Three different sizes of lead balls (.180, .250 & .330) are available to build Slinky weights from 1/8 ounce to 1 3/4 ounces.

Many rig fishermen enjoy tying their own leaders and snells. When tying walleye snells, stick with six or eight pound test line. I've found Stren's new High Impact Fluorocarbon leader material is the ideal material for tying walleye snells. Thin in diameter, extra strong and practically invisible underwater, this ex-

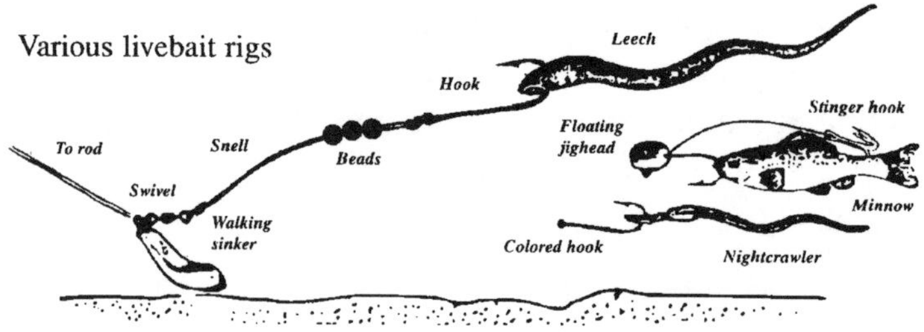

These variations show some of the common ways slip sinkers are used.

cellent product is far superior to snells tied using ordinary monofilament.

Any hook with a turned up eye can be easily snelled using fluorocarbon leader material. Begin by cutting the leader material to length and passing approximately one inch through the eye of the hook. Pinch the line against the shank of the hook and use the loose end to wind 6-10 wraps of leader around the shank of the hook.

Once the wraps are in place, pinch them securely in place and pass the end of the leader through the hook eye from the opposite direction. Pull the snell up tight and repeat the process if a second hook is to be added. Before tying off the snell add floats, beads or other attractors as needed then finish the snell with a double loop knot.

Making your own leaders allows the angler to custom tie rigs built with top quality line, hooks, beads, floats and other attractors. Extra leaders can be made and stored on a small chunk of foam or cardboard.

All of the versions of slip sinker rigging described above are best practiced with a graphite spinning rod and reel combination. The ideal rigging rod is six foot/six inches to seven foot long with a medium action. This rod balances best with a lightweight spinning reel loaded with six or eight pound test monofilament.

Armed with this equipment, rig fishermen will find it easier to tempt more bites and hook more fish. Bottom rigging may not be a totally new and improved way to tempt walleyes, but a few new twists on some old tactics have made rigging a better way than ever to catch walleyes when other methods fail.

In the next chapter we'll take a detailed look at the bottom bouncer. This unique rigging weight has taken the world of walleye fishing by surprise.

CHAPTER TIPS

1. Slip sinker rigging works best at ultra slow speeds. If you need to go faster, a bottom bouncer or other trolling sinker may be a better choice.

2. Bullet shaped weights like those used to fish plastic worms make ideal rigging weights when fishing in weed cover.

3. Rigging requires fresh and very lively bait. Change bait often and make sure to have at least two or three live bait choices available.

4. When rigging with leeches, choose a very light thin wire hook. Heavier hooks can prevent leeches from swimming naturally.

5. A medium size leech usually produces best, but large leeches can be deadly at times. Small leeches tend to attract too many panfish and other unwanted bites.

6. A two hook harness is ideal for rigging with crawlers. Be sure to space out the hooks at least six inches, so the second hook acts like a stinger.

Chapter 12

Bottom Bouncers

Two rod tips tapped out a signal like the Morse Code. The bobbing rods offered a clear message that a pair of crawler harnesses were hard at work searching for bottom hugging walleye. Suddenly one rod jabbed sharply downward, the tip smacking the water surface. The moment the rod was lifted free from its holder it was obvious the fish was a good one. Powerful head shakes and a stubborn reluctance to be pulled from bottom are the trade marks of trophy walleye.

Slowly the battle tilted in favor of the angler. After a couple gallant efforts to free itself the fish gave into the increasing pressure and allowed the net to slide under its body. The moment the net splashed home the fish erupted into a froth of spray and bubbles. The extra effort came too late to save this fish from the taxidermist.

Wherever walleye anglers gather, talk of suspended fish ultimately pops up. A hot topic featured in countless magazine articles and bait shop gossip, it's true that suspended populations of walleye are common in Great Lakes waters and beyond. Even many natural in-land lakes harbor suspended walleye if there's a pelagic (free swimming) forage base.

Despite this fact, the truth remains that walleye are far more

(Left) Bottom bouncers are rapidly becoming the most popular method of live bait rigging. This angler used an electric motor to position the boat and a spinner harness with a nightcrawler as bait.

apt to be found near bottom than suspended. Even in fisheries where these members of the perch family frequently suspend, the bottom is often the best place to be fishing.

Experienced walleye anglers use the bottom as a reference point from which to begin searching for walleye. If suspended fish start turning up on the graph, adjustments are made to take advantage of this bonanza.

Many walleye fishing methods are designed to present baits near the bottom, but none do it so efficiently as the common bottom bouncer.

A no nonsense method of walleye fishing, the common bottom bouncer sinker has a name that says it all. A "L" shaped piece of wire with a lead weight attached on the long arm and a snap swivel that accepts various leaders on the short arm. Nothing more, nothing less, these sinkers were designed to walk along the bottom while presenting a trailing spinner, live bait harness or crankbait in the face of waiting walleye. Used as trolling or drifting weights, bottom bouncers have an interesting place in the history of walleye fishing.

Made famous along the banks of the Missouri River in North and South Dakota, the bottom bouncer got its start when guides went looking for a bottom fishing method that man, woman and child could easily master. Guides and millions of other anglers found what they were looking for in the bottom bouncer and today there's hardly a corner of walleye country where these drifting and trolling weights aren't in common use.

Bottom bouncers weren't always so popular. Professional walleye anglers who traveled from tournament to tournament first introduced these fishing weights outside the Dakotas. It wasn't long before anglers in Minnesota, Wisconsin, Michigan, Ohio, Illinois and beyond were introduced to the fish catching magic of bottom bouncers.

I remember the first time I saw a bottom bouncer. I was assigned by what was then called Michigan Fisherman magazine to do a walleye story featuring the techiques of Bob Propst a

Scenes like this are common among anglers who fish bottom bouncers.

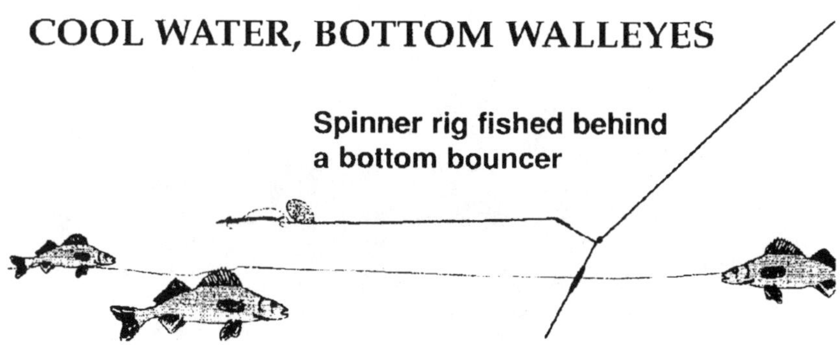

Spinner harnesses are the most popular snell used with bottom bouncerss. A spinner attracts walleye with color, flash, vibration and the alure of live bait.

touring walleye pro and South Dakota guide.

When Bob picked me up at the dock, his boat looked like a band of gypsies were living in it. Tackle, rods, bait boxes, life vests and about a dozen less useful items were scattered all over the boat. I struggled to find a place to sit.

I ended up sitting on a five gallon pail, which ironically was half filled with various sizes of strange wire sinkers Bob called bottom bouncers. He pointed to one of his rods he had rigged with a bottom bouncer and snelled spinner and told me to bait the harness with a nightcrawler.

Despite the fact that I had never fished a bottom bouncer before it didn't take long to discover why Bob suggested this method. We fished a large flat in the lower stretches of the Tittabawassee River. Bob slowly trolled upstream using a small gasoline kicker motor to keep the boat on course. We held the rods and used a slow pumping motion that pulled the spinner forward a few inches then dropped it back until the bottom bouncer could be felt hitting bottom.

When I got my first strike it simply felt like the rod got heavy. Not sure if I had hooked a walleye or an old plastic bag, I started reeling in to check my line. Soon as I lifted the fish off bottom it started to thrash and I realized I was indeed into a walleye. The fish came to net, we unhooked him, snapped a couple quick pictures and let it go.

Over and over again this process was repeated. Between us we caught a dozen or more walleyes in the first hour. After a couple fish I got the hang of detecting strikes and started hitting the fish with a solid sweeping hookset. By the time the day was over, I was begging Bob to let me have a few of his bottom bouncers.

Since that day I've fished the bottom bouncer religiously. Along the way I've added a trick or two of my own, but when it's all said and done, it's the design of the bottom bouncer itself that deserves the praise.

Only two hard fishing rules apply to bottom bouncers. These weights must to be fished at approximately a 45 degree angle from the boat to insure the sinker walks over the bottom and doesn't fall on its side. If too much line is let out the bottom bouncer will lay on its side and drag along the bottom where it is likely to snag and be lost.

When selecting bottom bouncers choose ones that are heavy enough to maintain bottom contact at the desired trolling or drifting speed. Bouncers range in size from 1/4 to four ounces. The most common sizes are 1/2, 1, 1-1/2 and 2 ounces. Keep in mind that it's better to fish a bouncer that's too heavy than one that's too light. The weights on some bottom bouncers are interchangeable making it a simple job to match the ideal bouncer weight to the fishing conditions at hand.

Leader length can also be a critical element of bottom bouncer fishing. The leader must not be so long that the trailing lure or live bait drags on bottom. The most productive leader lengths for bottom bouncer fishing is from 36-60 inches. Short leaders work best in dirty or off color water. Longer leaders are required in clear water.

A crawler harness (spinner) is the most common lure/live bait combination fished behind a bottom bouncer. Fished in shallow or deep water, spinners are hands down my favorite fish finding

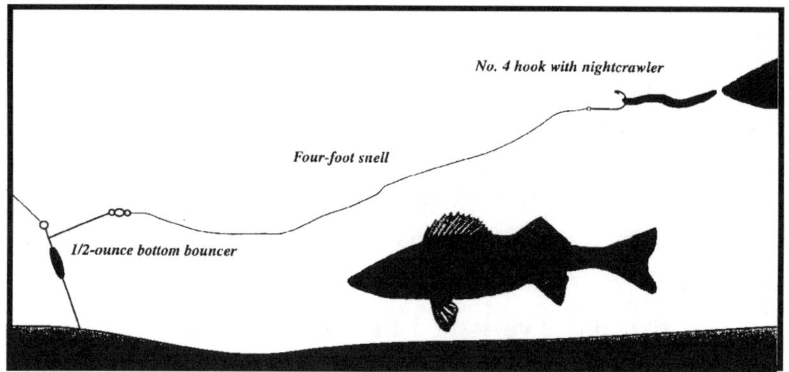

A bottom bouncer can be used with many different snell configurations. A single hook baited with a crawler or leech is a popular way to fish walleye, especially on northern lakes.

tool.

A spinning blade, be it a Colorado, Indiana, French, June Bug or other style, is a powerful fish attracting device. Combine the flash and vibration of a blade with the scent and natural action of a live crawler and it's easy to see why serious walleye anglers have so much faith in the bottom bouncer/spinner combination.

The Colorado and Indiana style blades are the most popular among walleye anglers. The rule of thumb is to start out with small blades and use larger ones when fish are active. The No. 1, 2 and 3 size blades are the mainstay of walleye fishing. When fish are active or if large fish are present I'll often switch to No. 4, 5 or 6 blades. In some extreme cases such as Lake Erie and other Great Lakes fisheries No. 7 and 8 blades are good choices.

Available in every color under the rainbow, walleye anglers need an assortment of blades in hammered silver, hammered brass, green, chartreuse and combinations of these patterns. I've discovered in recent years that my best producing blades are consistently genuine silver and gold plated. The extra flash these blades provide is a real advantage when fishing clear water Great Lakes fisheries. Silver and gold plated blades are more expensive than nickle or brass, but they are worth the few extra pennies they cost.

There's a common pitfall anglers who fish bouncer/spinner combinations often experience. Most anglers believe that various spinner blades have lift in the water when trolled. Actually the reverse is true. The dynamics of water moving over an object pulled through the water forces the object down. If the harness used is too long spinner rigs will simply drag on the bottom, even if the bouncer is positioned at the appropriate 45 degree angle.

If the harness drags on the bottom, the chances of snags are greatly increases, plus the bait isn't as readily visible or accessible to fish. When fishing bottom bouncer/spinner combinations check your rigs often. If the hooks pick up tiny pieces of bottom debris the harness is probably too long and needs to be shortened a little.

Commercially tied and packaged harnesses designed for use with bottom bouncers are available from most of the major tackle manufacturers. For the most part these harnesses are well suited to walleye fishing, but many anglers (myself included) prefer to tie custom harnesses in their spare time.

The harnesses I tie are considerably different than those available in tackle shops. I'm very particular about the hooks, line, floats and clevices I use on spinner rigs.

All my walleye harnesses start out with Stren's 12 pound test Hard Mono leader material. This super tough leader material is far more abrasive resistant than ordinary monofilament and also less visible in the water. Using Hard Mono leader makes for a harness that stands up to the abuse of walleye fishing.

During a tournament on Saginaw Bay last summer my partner Steve Holt and I caught over 60 walleye on our hand tied spinner rigs without a single harness breaking or failing in any way. Harnesses tied on normal monofilament rarely survive half a dozen fish before the line gets nicked and breaks. Usually the harness breaks at the worst possible moment.

The hooks I prefer for most spinner rigs are a thin wire turned up eye model 90774BLN produced by Mustad. My personal favorite is the No. 2, but many anglers prefer the smaller No. 4

size. These hooks are made of very light thin wire that sticks and holds walleye better than anything else I've tried. Also, because the hook is built on light wire, the hook can be bent and retrieved if it snags on bottom. Simply bend the hook back into shape, resharpen the hook and add fresh bait.

I use a standard Dupont snell to attach two of these hooks approximately six inches apart. The spacing of the hooks allows the back hook to be positioned midway in the crawler and helps to reduce short strikes.

Instead of glass or plastic beads, I often use foam floats to separate the hooks from the spinner blade. While floats do little or nothing to lift a spinner harness in the water, it's easier to thread a float on the leader than a dozen beads. Floats also add a little fish attracting color to the harness. It's a good idea to add one small bead before threading on the clevice. The clevice will turn against a bead more smoothly than against a foam float.

When it comes to attaching blades to spinner harnesses, the Quick Change clevice produced in Pierre, South Dakota is tops. This small plastic clevice allows blades to be quickly snapped on or off as need. Handy as a third hand this product makes changing blade size, shape or color second nature.

For most of my spinner fishing needs a harness 40-45 inches long is ideal. In very clear water a slightly longer leader may be needed.

A rarely practiced but deadly method of fishing bottom bouncer and spinner combinations involves the use of in-line planer boards such as the Off Shore Tackle Side-Planer. Side-Planers are a handy way of expanding trolling coverage when fishing spinners over large flats, reefs and other walleye structure.

To incorporate Side-Planers into a bottom bouncer program, simply set the bouncers as if they were flat lines and then attach the board to the line. When pulling bottom bouncers I recommend replacing the standard black OR14 release that comes on this board with a stronger spring tension OR16 (red) release. The extra spring tension insures that the board won't pop off the line if the bouncer or snell momentarily gets snagged on bottom.

Rigged in this manner a Side-Planer can be used to position two bottom bouncers per side. It's best to keep the boards within 50 feet of the boat to insure the bouncers run properly.

When a fish is hooked the struggling fish will pull the board backwards in the water. Simply reel in the board and fish together until the board comes within reach and can be removed from the line. Thanks to the pinch pad releases used on these boards it only takes a second to remove the board and continue fighting the fish.

While spinners are the most common terminal tackle used with bottom bouncers, these unique weights are also well suited to fishing with a plain leader and single hook. Whenever I think of a bottom bouncer and clean snell, I think of Canada. The type of fishing often encountered in natural lakes throughout much of Canada is ideally suited to a bottom bouncer armed with a single hook and snell. The bait of choice is a lively medium leech.

This classic summer time presentation is best suited to deep water structure so common in Canadian Shield lakes. Sunken islands and rock reefs are among the most common places to find mid summer walleye.

One of my favorite ways to fish this structure is with a boat equipped with an electric motor and dependable sonar unit. My standard method of fishing involves cruising the tops of structure while watching the graph carefully for signs of fish. Once I locate fish, I break out a rod equipped with a bottom bouncer, 48-inch snell and No. 4 Mustad Finesse hook. Leeches are the bait of choice. Crawers can be effective at times.

This rig is lowered to bottom and using the electric motor I slowly scoot around the structure ticking bottom with the sinker in a touch and go manner. I rarely drag the bottom bouncer, instead preferring to use the weight to keep tabs on the bottom and make sure my trailing bait is fishing close to bottom.

Fishing a leech and bottom bouncer is a slow presentation. If the leech is pulled too fast it will simply spin in the water and offer none of the irrestible wiggling action leeches are known for.

If the water is 15 feet deep or deeper it's usually possible to locate fish on the graph and then position your bait right in front of these fish. Sometimes it takes several passes to tempt a strike. Other times the walleye jump on the leech the second it comes within reach.

When you feel a bite, slowly drop the rod tip back in order to give yourself a full swinging motion and set the hook with a strong forward sweep of the rod. Light or medium action baitcasting tackle equipped with eight or 10 pound test monofilament is ideal for this style of fishing.

The rod needs to be fairly light and handy because the angler holds the rod constantly. This technique can also be accomplished with a fairly stiff spinning rod.

Effective in natural lakes, reservoirs, rivers and the Great Lakes the bottom bouncer has rapidly become a "must have" piece of tackle for the walleye angler. In the next chapter we'll examine three way rigs and explain when and how to use this rigging option.

CHAPTER TIPS

1. When hand holding a bottom bouncer a light graphite triggerstick equipped with a baitcasting reel works best. When trolling, heavier rods such as a downrigger rod and line-counter style reel is a good option.

2. When fishing spinner harnesses behind a bottom bouncer, be sure to use the plastic Quick Change clevices. These unique clevices allow anglers to change blade size, shape and color in seconds, making spinner fishing much easier.

3. Bottom bouncers range in size from 1/4 ounce to four ounces. The most commonly used sizes include 1/2, 1, 1.5 and 2 ounce models.

MAGNA

MARINER
Chapter

Three-Way Rigs

Three way rigging is a presentation with a lot of faces. Depending on which part of walleye wonderland you're fishing a three way rig could be a river trolling system, a rig used to fish wing dams or a Great Lakes trolling system designed to pattern aggressive suspended walleye. The variations used in three way rigging boggle the mind. In fact about the only thing many of these rigs have in common is the swivel!

Despite the many forms of three way rigging, when most anglers think of three ways the classic Wolf River rig comes to mind. An unique bottom rig designed for trolling in swift current, the classic Wolf River rig features a main line tied to a three way swivel. Attached to the remaining swivels are a short dropper line that leads to a lead sinker and a longer leader that attaches to one of many different live bait or artificial lure combinations.

When I was competing on the Masters Walleye Council trail years ago, the Mississippi River was one of my favorite destinations. Like all rivers water levels on the Mississippi are constantly fluctuating. One year in particular heavy spring rains and snow melt left the river a swollen mess complete with ice cold water, fast current and muddy water. The three demons of river fishing, I knew at one glance that fishing main river structure such as wing dams, channel

(Left) Rick Smith of Escanaba Michigan used a three way rig to bump bottom in deep clear waters of Little Bay de Noc.

edges and day markers would be out of the question.

The slowest moving water I could find was along a flooded bank where buckbrush stood in about two foot of water. Just outside the flooded brush the river bed dipped down a couple feet, forming a little ledge with some rip rap, gravel and a few stones scattered along the bottom.

I originally found fish at this spot by drifting downstream and casting jigs to shore, but it became apparent that with a rising current casting jigs was going to be a tough row to hoe. Instead I decided to troll upstream using my electric motor. The current was too swift to use a jig, so I decided on a Wolf River rig. To one swivel I attached the main line, to another I attached a 12-inch dropper leading to an one ounce pencil sinker. On the remaining swivel I tied a four foot leader armed with a single Aberdeen hook, dressed with a plastic twister tail grub and a leech.

Using a bow mount electric motor I slowly made my way upstream, tunking the sinker on the bottom every few feet. My first fish came quickly. A two pound sauger jumped on the twister tail/leech combination and was soon brought to net. Within an hour I'd nursed another sauger and three walleye from a spot not much wider than my boat and only about 100 feet long.

On the very same day a number of good fishermen I hang out with struggled to fish the main current. They all came up empty handed. When river fishing conditions are tough, the three way rig is one of the first systems I opt for.

Since that day on the Mississippi, I've used these versatile rigs to fish high and/or muddy water many times. The basic rig I described can be modified to include a heavy jig on the bottom in place of the pencil sinker. Using a jig on the bottom adds another hook to the presentation and the chance to land a bonus fish or two.

Before fishing a three way with a jig on bottom, check your state fishing regulations. This style of rigging is not allowed in some states and in others this rig is considered two lines.

What's used at the business end of a three way rig can also be modified. The twister tail/leech on a No. 1 or 2 Aberdeen hook is one of the most popular and versatile combinations. In clear to slightly stained water natural color twister tails work best. In turbid or muddy water the brighter the plastic bait used the better.

It also helps to glue the twister tail in place using a drop or two of Super Glue. These rigs must be made ahead of time so the glue has plenty of time to dry and set up.

A minnow can easily be substituted for the leech and if desired a stinger hook added to hook light biters. Other styles of plastic baits such as shad bodies, twin tail grubs and curl tail worms can also be used effectively with this rig.

A two hook spinner harness baited with a fat nightcrawler is another excellent three way rigging option. In river current a smaller blade such as a No. 1 or 2 Colorado or Indiana is usually the best choice.

Another option is to put away live bait and use a shallow diving crankbait such as a No. 7, 9 or 11 floating Rapala, Baby Storm ThunderStick or a small Rebel Minnow. Crankbaits should be fished on a 48-60 inch monofilament leader.

The Illinois River MWC tournament held each year in early April is routinely won by teams trolling the flats using a three way rig and a shallow diving crankbait. The normal method is to troll upstream just fast enough to make headway against the current.

Another popular three way rigging option incorporates crankbaits and the new super braid lines. Because the super braids are so thin in diameter, they are ideal for three way rigging in rivers. The thinner line makes it easier to maintain contact with bottom while using less weight. This no stretch line also makes it easier to feel bottom and bites, especially when fishing in deep water.

When rigging with super lines, tie the main line directly to the three way swivel. The 10 pound test versions offer line diameter similar to six pound test monofilament, yet they are much tougher. The dropper line should be tied using six or eight pound test monofilament to a pencil or bass casting style sinker. If the sinker snags up, simply tug on the line until the sinker breaks off, then tie on another sinker.

The leader to the lure should be 48-60 inches long and made of eight pound test monofilament. A small snap can be used at the terminal end to make changing crankbaits easier. Shallow diving stickbaits are the ideal choice for this three way rigging method. Some excellent choices include the Fred Arbogast Snooker, Storm Jr. ThunderStick, Bomber Long A, Smithwick Rattlin' Rogue, Bagley Bang-O-Lure, Mann's Minus One and Reef Runner RipStick.

An ideal rig for fishing deep or swift river current, three way rigs that incorporate super braid lines can easily be fished along bottom in waters up to 30 or 40 feet deep. The ideal presentation is to slow troll upstream just fast enough to make headway against the current. Depending on current speed this trolling method may call for an electric motor or a small gasoline kicker.

When a fish is hooked trolling upstream, put the boat in neutral and drift downstream while fighting the fish. If the boat continues to pull upstream, it's easy to put too much pressure on the fish and tear the hooks free.

Not all three way rigs are used in river current. Great Lakes trollers are fond of trolling rigs that incorporate a crankbait and spinner or crankbait and spoon combination. Trolling two lure options at once is an excellent way to determine which lures walleye prefer on any given day.

Open water three way trolling rigs normally use a diving style crankbait as a means of pulling a spoon or spinner to depth. Most anglers favor the crankbait rigged on the bottom using a short 24 inch leader. A 36-60 inch leader is run to a lightweight flutter spoon or a spinner/crawler combination. The spinner or spoon is run on a longer lead so it doesn't interfere with the crankbait.

Strong diving crankbaits are ideal for this three-way rigging option. The Storm 3/8 ounce Rattle Tot, Luhr Jensen Hot Lips, Mann's Stretch 15, Cotton Cordell Wally Diver and Rapala Rattlin' Fat Rap, are among my favorites.

When spoons get the nod, down sized models are usually the most productive. Some of the best choices in the Great Lakes include the Bait Rigs Walleye Willow Spoon, Wolverine Silver Streak, Fred

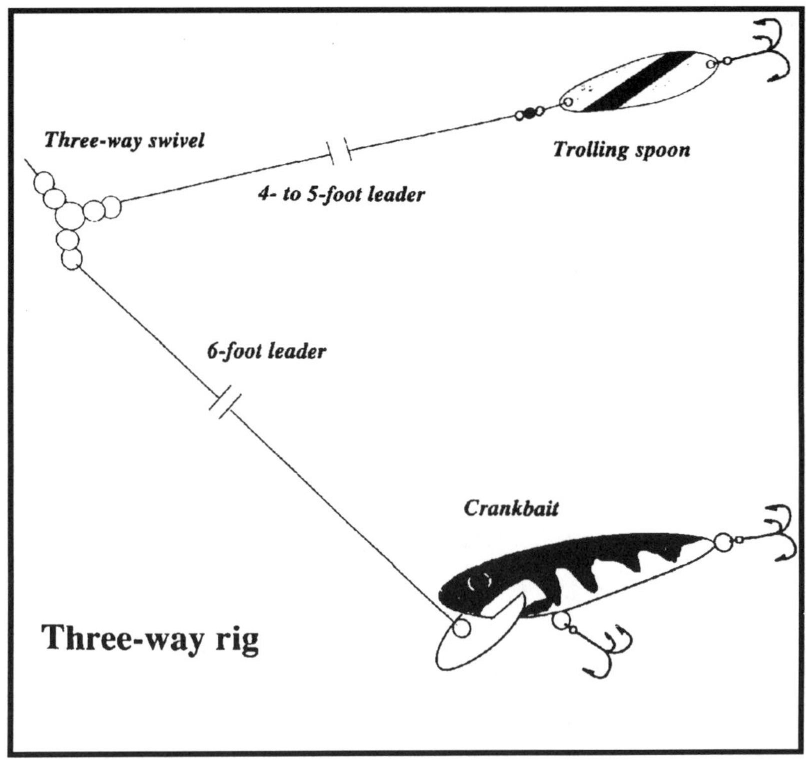

Using a crankbait and spoon together is one of the most popular forms of three way trolling.

Arbogast Doctor Spoon, Stinger, Luhr Jensen Needle Fish and Alpena Diamond.

Spinner harnesses baited with crawlers are also a popular choice for three way trolling rigs. Small Colorado and Indiana style blades are the best choice.

When setting lines equipped with rigs, be sure to let the lures back slowly and smoothly. If the lure is let back too quickly, the crankbait can easily tangle in the spoon or spinner line.

I've seen many times when three way rigs like those described here produce two fish at once! Usually it's either the spoon, spinner or crankbait that produces best. If the spoon or spinner produces best, I'll usually switch to a different trolling technique such as snap weight trolling that allows me to fish strictly spoons or spinners. If the crankbait produces most of the bites, I'll usually remove the three way rigs and troll straight cranks behind planer boards.

Another Great Lakes three way rig is often used in place of a bottom bouncer and spinner. Early and late in the season Great Lakes walleye are often found on deep water mud flats. Fish can be found holding in 30-50 feet of water and usually their fins are touching the soft bottom.

On Lake Erie I've seen where three-ways will out fish bottom bouncers two to one. This is especially true right after the spawn when large females can be found cruising on the mud flats in 30-40 feet of water. The presentation has to be slow and the bait positioned only a couple inches off bottom to interest these fish. If a bottom bouncer is used it must be set perfectly to prevent the bouncer from tipping over and dragging in the mud. What often happens is the harness drags on bottom and gets quickly fouled with zebra mussels.

Three way rigs have a little less drag in the water and are easier to fish tight to bottom structure. Also, there's no limit to the weight that can be used with a three way, whereas bottom bouncers are tough to find in the three and four ounce sizes.

The best way to fish these heavy three way rigs is with a downrigger style rod equipped with a line counter reel and 10-12 pound test monofilament. It's critical to set the boat speed before setting lines. Usually the slowest speed that will spin the Colorado or Indiana blade is the best choice.

Zero out the line counter and let the three way rig free spool to bottom. When the weight hits bottom put your thumb on the reel spool and let the boat troll forward a few yards. As the boat moves forward the line will angle backwards. Lower the rod tip to feel for the bottom. If you can't feel the bottom let out a little more line until the sinker can easily be felt hitting bottom.

Once the sinker is set to tick bottom every few feet, put the rod in a conveniently located rod holder and set another line. Note the number on the line counter reel and set additional lines accordingly.

When fishing this unique three way rig, two anglers can position four rods for precise bottom trolling. The lines should be checked every few minutes to insure that zebra mussels haven't fouled the

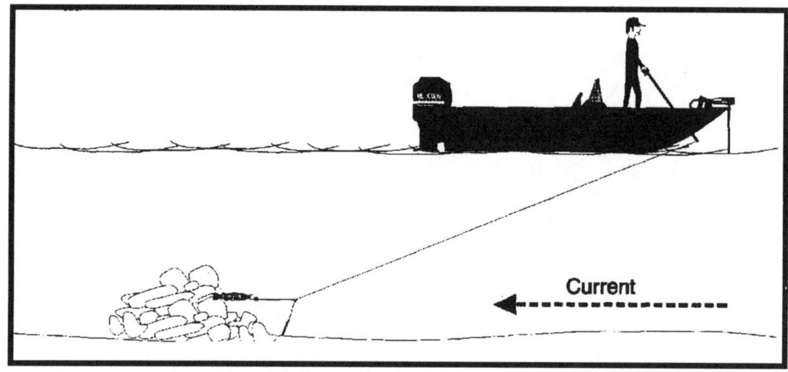

In flowing water three way rigs are often used to fish rock piles, wing dams, channel edges and other river structure.

hooks. A 40-45 inch leader works very well for this style of fishing.

If the fish are inactive small No. 1, 2 or 3 blades work best. When the fish become a little more active larger No. 4, 5 or 6 blades will produce consistent action and often trophy sized fish.

When fishing keep a close eye on the sonar unit. At the first sign of fish suspending a foot or two off the bottom, bring your three way rigs up a reel turn or two. When walleye start suspending over the mud flats they are usually in a biting mood. Some of the biggest walleye I catch every year are taken using this simple rigging method.

The three way rigging options outlined here are just the tip of the iceberg. There are as many ways to fish these rigs as anglers who enjoy using them.

In the next chapter we'll discuss the most simple of all live bait rigs the split shot rig. This versatile rig can be casted, dragged, fished in current, still water, through snag filled areas and it even makes for an excellent way to fish a dead rod.

Chapter 14

Split Shot Rigs

Simple and unsophisticated, an ordinary split shot pinched on the line a couple feet in front of a single hook constitutes a live bait rig. Crude by many standards, let there be no doubt split shot rigs have a time and place. The most simple of live bait rigs is one of the most effective.

As a tournament fisherman, I use split shot rigs frequently. Developing confidence in this simple presentation is the first step. I frequently fish split shot rigs because for one, they're easy to rig and can be effective in a wide variety of situations. Secondly, a split shot rig is the only live bait rig that can be casted effectively. Thirdly, a split shot rig is the ideal choice when fishing a dead rod in combination with other walleye fishing presentations.

Fashioning a split shot rig takes less time than tying your shoes! Ideally suited to spinning tackle, split shotting works best when matched up to light or medium/light action spinning rods and six to eight pound test line.

Begin by tying a single hook, floating jighead or soft body jig directly to the monofilament. Complete the rig by pinching a split shot on the line 18-24 inches ahead of the hook. Use just enough split shot weight to keep the rig on bottom.

(Left) The most simple of all live bait rigs, a split shot rig can be cast, dragged or fished as a dead rod rig.

The bait to be used dictates the best hook choice. For fishing minnows a No. 1 or 2 Aberdeen is always a good choice. Mustad also has a new hook the 90774BLN that is made of thin wire with a turned up eye for snelling. Both these hooks penetrate quickly with minimal pressure.

If leeches are the bait of choice, choose the lightest possible hook. One of Mustad's Walleye Snells (515WES) in size 4 is a good choice. This hook comes snelled on a 7 foot clear monofilament leader. Simply cut the leader to the desired length. Other suitable hooks include the Eagle Claw Featherlite series L757G Walleye and Owner 5230 Walleye Snell. Each of these hooks are light enough that the leech can swim naturally. Most other hooks will weigh down the leech and reduce it's delicate action.

Most crawler fishermen prefer a beak style hook like Mustad's 92567R, VMC's 7299, Gamakatsu's 021 or Eagle Claw's L195G. This compact hooks are easy to hide in a crawler and insure the bait has a natural undulating action in the water. Choose the size 4 or 2.

Some anglers prefer a floating jighead or soft body jig such as the Phelps Floater when fishing split shot rigs. These unique hooks add color and bulk to the presentation and can be helpful especially in stained or turbid water. The No. 4 size is best for crawlers and leeches and the No. 2 a better choice when fishing minnows.

The design of a split shot rig allows them to be casted from a boat or shore. When casting a split shot rig, it helps to think of this presentation as a jigging method rather than rigging.

Where split shot rigs have an advantage over leadheads is in snag filled waters. Because the hook and bait are free to move about on the short leader, a split shot rig can be worked through rocks, wood and weeds with far less hang-ups than leadheads that position the weight, hook and bait on bottom.

The biggest mistake anglers make when fishing split shot rigs is over working the presentation. Concentrate on moving the rig

Keith Kavajecz took this walleye using nothing more than a hook, split shot and night crawler.

slowly so the bait can swim naturally and tease strikes from waiting walleye.

Make a short cast and let the split shot sink to bottom. When the line collapses on the surface that's your signal that the bait has hit bottom. Reel up the slack line carefully until you can just feel the weight of the shot on bottom. With the rod at the 10 O'clock position and pointed at the split shot, pull the rod towards you until it reaches the 11 O'clock position and hold the rod still for a few seconds. This rod motion will lift the split shot slightly off bottom and cause it to swing towards you in a pendulum motion.

Next reel back down to the 10 O'clock position and pick up the slack line until the weight of the split shot can be felt again. Repeat the process by pulling the rod to the 11 O'clock position, holding for a few seconds and reeling up the slack again. Continue this process over and over again until the rig has been completely retrieved.

This simple jigging motion keeps a slight tension in the line that makes it possible to detect strikes. Remember, the best way to fish a split shot rig is on a taunt, but not tight line. A taunt line will telegraph even the most subtle strike. If slack is allowed to form in the line, strikes are very difficult to detect.

Keep the jigging motion simple and when a strike is detected, set the hook immediately using a strong upwards rod sweep. Unlike other rigging methods where the angler feeds line to the fish, split shotting calls for a quick and decisive hookset.

I routinely use a split shot rig as a second line while fishing a different lure, bait or presentation with à primary rod. Known as dead rod fishing, the split shot rig is baited, casted out, placed in a rod holder and forgotten until a bucking rod tip signals a strike.

Fishing with a dead rod may seem like the lazy man's method, but actually it makes it possible to experiment with two different presentations at the same time. Think of zeroing in on walleyes like a hunter sights in a rifle. The hunter test fires his rifle at a target, adjusts his sights accordingly and fires again. The process

The beauty of split shot rigs is they can be fished in areas that would eat up jigs. These anglers are casting to flooded timber.

of shooting test shots and making necessary adjustments continues until the bullet strikes the bulls eye. Trying different baits, lures, and presentations is the on going process required to find and pattern walleye.

Dead rods and split shot rigs work best in areas where snags are minimal. Sand, clay and gravel flats are good places to experiment with split shot rigs. Small reefs are also good places to try out a dead rod.

A few years ago while pre-fishing for a tournament I encountered piles of 3-5 pound walleye using a shallow water reef. The reef topped off in about eight feet of water and was covered with pea sized gravel and boulders the size of a basketball. Casting a 1/8 ounce jig tipped with a fathead minnow produced one walleye after another. Unfortunately, jigging is a rather slow paced technique that limits the angler to one rod.

In an effort to put two lines in the water and maximize my catch, I set out a split shot rig baited with a large minnow on a dead rod. During the course of the day the dead rod only produced about half a dozen fish. Fortunately, one of the fish landed was my largest of the day. The kicker fish I earned by split shotting kept me in the money at a tournament where ounces often add up to dollars.

Other areas where a dead rod are handy include rivers with slow to moderate currents and contour trolling along breaklines in natural lakes or reservoirs.

Longer (8'-12') steelhead style rods are the ideal split shotting tool when fishing a dead line. Noodle rods such as the Browning Syntec and Midas Dick Swan series are ideal for dead rod fishing. These long and soft action rods help present the bait a little further from the boat and the light tip action also telegraphs strikes readily.

Many times I've seen a dead rod out fish other presentations where the angler held the rod. One such experience happened to me while fishing the Tittabawasse River in Saginaw County. I was fishing in early May during the annual spawning run. A common technique here is to drift river flats using split shot rigs and jigs tipped with crawlers for bait.

A simple way to fish, the boat is positioned perpendicular to the current flow and allowed to drift naturally downstream. The rigs and jigs are casted upstream and allowed to sink to bottom. The key is to let out enough line so the rig or jig drags along bottom.

On this particular day I chose to cast a jig with one rod while dragging a split shot rig on a second dead rod. Despite my best efforts I couldn't buy a bite casting a jig. Meanwhile, the dead rod with the split shot rig had a fish on almost constantly. Figuring it had to be the split shot rig the fish wanted, I decided to cast the split shot and let the jig simply drag along bottom for awhile. You guessed it, the jig started producing fish after fish, meanwhile the split shot rig I was casting shut off as quickly as a spring shower.

When I finally wised up and let both rods simply fish as dead rods, the action was so fast I could hardly keep baited lines in the water. If there's a moral to this story it's don't think that just because the rod is in your hand it will catch more fish!

The versatile split shot rig is one of the least used live bait rigs among walleye anglers, yet in my humble opinion it's one of the best. Simple to rig and simple to fish, the next time you reach for a jig or slip sinker rig, ask yourself if a split shot rig might be a better choice.

In the next chapter we'll tackle a new rigging system known as Snap Weights. This in-line trolling system has many live bait rigging options.

CHAPTER TIPS

1. Split shotting is an ideal rigging method for fishing in snag filled waters. Use a soft wire Aberdeen style hook that can be bent out and recovered if it snags bottom. Once the hook is recovered, simply bend it back into shape, sharpen it and add fresh bait.

2. A split shot rig works great as a dead rod fishing system when casting a jig or crankbait on a primary line.

3. When using split shot rigs, use just enough weight to keep the bait on bottom. Using too much weight will lead to unnecessary snags.

4. A split shot rig can be cast, dragged or drifted making it one of the most versatile of all live bait rigs.

Chapter 15

Snap Weight Rigging

If you want to catch more walleye, get in-line! Interest in walleye fishing has exploded across the Midwest, sending anglers onto the water buzzing with new and better angling methods.

One of the latest ways to tempt a walleye into biting involves an in-line trolling sinker developed by none other than yours truly. Dubbed Snap Weights, these unique trolling sinkers are manufactured by Off Shore Tackle and are an easy and popular way to add weight to any fishing line.

The idea for Snap Weights came to me while fishing trout on Lake Michigan. I was fishing a common rig known as a lead drop line. A jettison style release is used to hold a heavy (one pound) lead ball on the fishing line. When a fish is hooked the jettison release opens up and drops the lead ball, leaving the angler to fight the fish without fighting the weight.

I reasoned that lead drop lines would work equally well on walleye, but dropping lead into the water is both expensive and a bad environmental policy. Fortunately, when walleye fishing the weights needed to achieve the common fishing depths aren't excessive.

(Left) Kurt Beckstrom of North American Fisherman magazine trolled up this walleye using a crankbait and snap weight combination.

It didn't take me long to try out my idea using some make shift trolling weights fashioned from downrigger releases and bell sinkers. I made a trip to Little Bay de Noc and went to work fishing the deep water basin near the town of Gladstone. My first fishing attempts were with crawler harnesses. I let out 10-20 feet of lead, attached the weight and let out additional line until I could feel the weight hitting bottom.

Much to my excitement the snap-on weight idea worked! I started catching walleye in 20, 30, 40 and even 50 feet of water! When I experimented a little more I discovered that the farther I placed the weight from the lure, the better the system worked.

Excited about my idea, I contacted long time friend and trolling expert Bruce DeShano of Off Shore Tackle. Bruce looked over my crude trolling sinkers, raised his eyebrows and went to work refining my idea. Within weeks we were fishing with prototype Snap Weights fashioned from OR10 planer board releases equipped with extra heavy tension springs. The heavy spring tension insured that the weight wouldn't pop off the line when fighting a fish.

A short time later Off Shore Tackle introduced the OR16 Snap Weight release and a Snap Weight kit complete with four releases, and an assortment of 1/2, 3/4, 1, 1.5, 2 and 3 ounce weights. Within one year every walleye professional on the PWT trail was fishing this new in-line trolling weight and half a dozen tackle manufacturers were copying our idea with similar products.

Today, the words Snap Weights are used so much in walleye fishing circles they have become a generic term rather than the brand name it was intended to be. Brown trout, steelhead, salmon and trout fishermen are also jumping on the band wagon.

Ideally suited to trolling snelled spinners, Snap Weight have added a new dimension to live bait rigging. Like other trolling sinkers, Snap Weights come in different sizes. Weights ranging in size from 1/2 ounce to eight ounces are attached to an OR16 (red) pinch pad style line release via a split ring. Snap Weights are attached to the fishing line by pinching open the release with a thumb and forefinger and sliding the line between the rubber

The author frequently uses snap weights when fishing spinners in open water.

pads. Snap Weights feature a heavy spring tension that holds the sinker securely on the line. When a fish is hooked, the angler fights the fish as normal and simply removes the weight when it's retrieved to within reach.

Using snap-on weights opens up a lot of trolling options for the walleye fisherman. Unlike bottom bouncers, keel sinkers, split shots, slip sinkers, and other fishing weights, snap-on weights aren't permanently attached to the line.

A snap-on weight can be positioned anywhere between the lure and rod tip. This simple feature allows anglers to use longer trolling leads than possible with sinker styles that must be permanently attached to the fishing line and allows weight to be easily added to any lure for increased trolling depth.

The longer leads possible with snap-on weights allows the lure more freedom of movement (action) and separates the lure from unnatural objects that may spook walleye, ie: trolling sinkers or diving planes.

Applications for Snap Weights are popping up almost as fast as dandelions in June. These unique sinkers are ideal for trolling near bottom structure or for walleye suspended in the water column.

Of all the options available to anglers using snap-on weights, fishing spinners for suspended walleye has become one of the most popular. Consistently catching suspended or open walleye is one of the greatest trolling challenges. Unlike their counterparts that become structure loving home bodies, open water walleye wander endlessly.

When most anglers think of suspended walleye, they conjure up images of Lake Erie, Saginaw Bay and the other Great Lakes fisheries. Walleye are actually found suspended in a wide variety of waters. Any natural lake or reservoir that supports a population of walleye and a pelagic (free roaming/suspended) forage base is likely to provide a suspended walleye fishery. Many of these fisheries offer unlimited fishing opportunities for those anglers who know where and how to tap into it.

This illustration shows how anglers use snap weights to fish for suspended walleye using spinner harnesses.

Pelagic baitfish including smelt, alewife, gizzard shad, thread fin shad, emerald shiners, ciscoes and young-of-the-year drum are the preferred forage of walleye. When these species are present in a body of water, walleye often forsake all other food sources to dine on these protein rich fishes.

Forever in pursuit of wandering baitfish, open water walleye are in some respects prisoners of their chosen food source. Ironically, the baitfish walleye depend on are in turn held captive by the floating plankton that supports this food chain.

Wind and waves drift clouds of plankton around open water basins like a weather balloon. Wherever the plankton drifts, baitfish follow and schools of suspended walleye are never far behind.

Because open water walleye wander endlessly, anglers must search them out each day on the water. Fortunately suspended walleye tend to be found in mid-lake basins or flats that feature water 20 to 50 feet deep.

"It doesn't make sense to waste valuable time fishing until fish are located, says charter captain Al Lesh. "Approach open water basins by dividing the water up into manageable pieces."

To avoid the overwhelming feeling of looking for a needle in

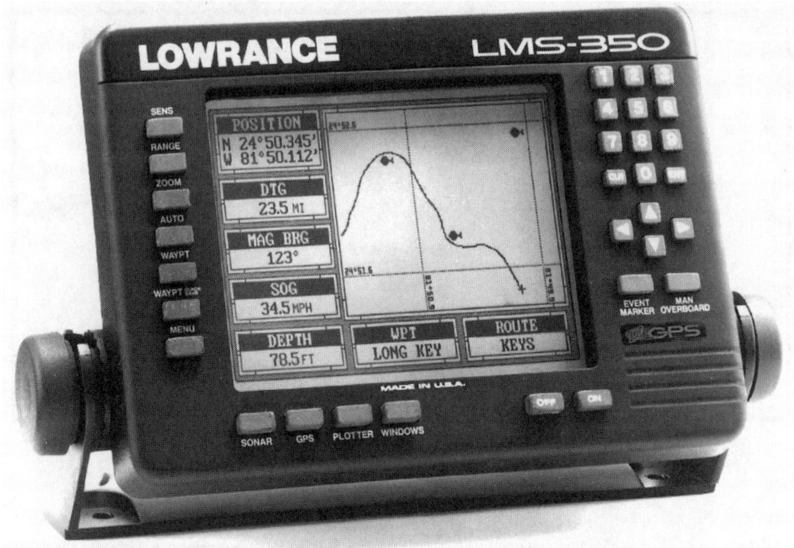

The Lowrance 350A is considered by many to be the best graph/GPS plotter available.

a hay stack, try searching out open water by running at a high rate of speed for a few hundred yards then slowing down and watching the graph for a few hundred yards. This run awhile/ watch awhile approach eliminates unproductive water quickly.

"The boat must be slowed down to effectively mark fish," adds Lesh. "Slowing the boat down reduces turbulence created by the hull cutting through the water and helps the graph show a clear picture of what's beneath the boat. For the best results the boat should be moving less than six miles per hour."

When hunting for suspended fish quality electronics are a must. A high resolution liquid crystal readout LCR graph such as Lowrance's 350A or X-85 is ideal for locating walleye suspended in the water column. Once walleye are located, it takes more than a fishing graph to stay on these open water fish. A Global Positioning System (GPS) unit provides the navigation aid to make repeated trolling passes on fish found far from shoreline markings.

Available in both permanently mounted units and hand-held portables, GPS technology is becoming more affordable each year.

Units range in price from $200.00 to $1,000.00.

Models equipped with a graphics plotter such as the 350A are very popular. Like a road map, a plotter screen shows the current location of the boat, where it has traveled, plus saved waypoints or icons that represent important points of interest. Armed with this kind of technology, it's easy to return to productive fishing waters or find your way back to port even in fog or darkness.

More sophisticated mapping units are even easier to use and they show much more detail. The Lowrance Global Map 2000 is the unit all others are compared to. This state-of-the-art machine accepts mini-map cartridges known as smart maps. Smart map cartridges are available for most major fishing areas in the United States and Canada. Each of these maps contains very detailed information including depth contour lines, landmarks, shipping channels, etc.

Mapping units have one huge advantage over plotter units. When using a mapping GPS unit, it's possible to navigate to areas without the benefit of known waypoints or latitude/longitude coordinates. With a plotter unit, a known location is needed before navigation can begin. Summed up in terms an angler can understand, mapping units make it possible to explore areas that are uncharted on most fishing maps with ease and safety.

Quality fishing electronics and GPS units are an absolute necessity when fishing open water walleye. Once a school of fish are located, take a waypoint reading or save an icon to mark the location of the fish and prepare to make an initial trolling run.

One fact of trolling always holds true; it's easier to troll with the wind than against it. This is especially true when trolling slowly or when fishing in rough seas.

To set up the first trolling run, motor straight upwind 1/4 to 1/2 mile, turn around and troll straight at the coordinates where fish were located. Start setting lines and keep an eye on the GPS unit to insure the boat is heading straight for the waypoint where the fish are waiting.

In open water situations, it's important to troll as closely as possible to waypoints. Keep in mind that the accuracy of GPS mapping and plotter units varies depending on if and when the federal government scrambles the satellite signals.

In the interest of national defense GPS satellite signals are often scrambled reducing navigation accuracy down to about 100 meters on the average. The scrambling process is called selective availability. If the satellite signals aren't altered the accuracy of these units can be as good as three meters! Alas, sometime during the next 10 years the government promises to do away with their selective availability policy and let fishermen fish! Until then GPS is still the best game in town.

Snelled spinners (harnesses baited with nightcrawlers) are becoming one of the most popular trolling lures used to catch suspended walleye. Spinners and snap-on weights are an ideal marriage. Depending on the amount of weight used and the trolling speed selected, spinners can be fished from inches below the surface to 40 feet deep with ease.

A walleye spinner combines a thumping Colorado or Indiana style blade, fish attracting flash and smell of live bait into an irresistible combination for hungry walleye. Unfortunately, most commercially packaged spinners are designed to be used with bottom bouncers and are not suited to open water trolling.

Serious open water anglers build their own spinners. Instead of using the baitholder style hooks on most spinners, they snell two No. 4 treble hooks onto a short length of 12-20 pound test Stren Hard Mono leader. Tough like the bristles of a nylon brush, this unique leader material holds up to toothy critters like walleye much better than harnesses tied using monofilament. Treble hooks are selected because they bite and hold better than single hooks, especially on the large and powerful fish often encountered when open water trolling.

The overall spinner length need not be more than 12-18 inches long. Since the spinner is attached to the terminal end of the fishing line and trolled far behind the boat, long spinners simply aren't necessary and the shorter versions are easier to store and keep untangled.

The treble hooks should be snelled approximately four to six inches apart. This hook configuration allows the front hook to be placed through the nose of the crawler and the back hook to easily reach into the mid section of a jumbo nightcrawler. Spacing out the hooks reduces short strikes and yields more landed fish.

Once the hooks are tied in place, add half a dozen colorful beads and one of the Quick Change plastic clevices that allow spinner blades to be easily clipped on or taken off. Using a Quick Change spinner clevices permits the angler to switch blade size, style and color in seconds without re-tying.

The most common spinner blades are Colorado and Indiana styles. Sizes ranges from three to eight are used in open water trolling situations. Stick with the smaller blades in tough conditions and use progressively larger blades when the fish are biting well or if big fish are the target.

The best colors include hammered silver, hammered brass, chartreuse, green, orange and combinations of these colors. Genuine silver and gold plated blades are also an excellent investment. These highly polished blades provide far more flash than nickel or brass.

Open water spinners are completed by securing a barrel style ball bearing swivel to the tag end. Ball bearing swivels are a must to help eliminate annoying line twist when trolling spinners.

The open water spinners described above combine the flash and natural scent of a spinner rig with the hooking success of a crankbait. Use the largest crawlers available for best results.

Different size Snap Weights are used to present spinners at various trolling depths. The most common rigging method calls for a spinner set 50 feet behind the boat. Once the spinner is set behind the boat, place a snap-on weight onto the line and let out an additional 50 feet of line. The snap-on weight sinks, pulling the spinner down with it.

Known as the 50/50 system this line can be trolled flat behind the boat or attached to an in-line planer board such as the Off Shore Tackle Side-Planer and taken to the side of the boat for additional lure coverage.

On the initial trolling pass set up with several lines that present a variety of spinner blade types, sizes and colors at different depth ranges. Offering a smorgasborg of baits helps to pattern the fish quickly. Once a successful pattern emerges, simply duplicate the pattern with additional lines set up the same way.

This trolling technique calls for medium action tackle and 10-14 pound test monofilament. Graphite/fiberglass composite or fiberglass downrigger style rods are the ideal choice for most walleye trolling applications. These rods are half the cost of graphite versions plus they are less fragile and forgiving of rough handling.

Monitoring the amount of trolling lead used is critical to this style of fishing. Many anglers use reels with built in line counter devices to determine how much lead is being used. Line counters that attach to the rod are also available. Still others prefer to use metered fishing lines that have a color band or mark every 10 feet. By counting the color marks as they pass by the rod tip, it's easy to determine exact trolling leads and later duplicate the effective ones.

The advent of the Snap Weight is having a dramatic impact on open water walleye fishing. When you combine these popular in-line weights with the garden variety crawler harness, the result is something you have to see to believe. For me it's been a real thrill watching an idea as simple as Snap Weights become so popular. It has also been a thrill catching fish that until a few years ago we were mostly missing out on.

In chapter 16 we'll look at the world of jigging spoons. These versatile lures can be casted or jigged vertically with equal success.

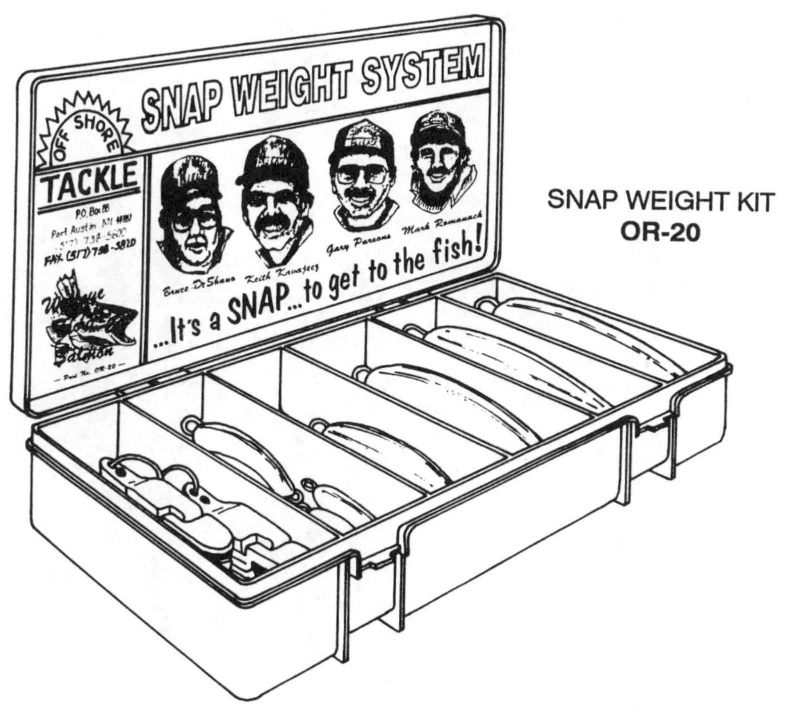

SNAP WEIGHT KIT
OR-20

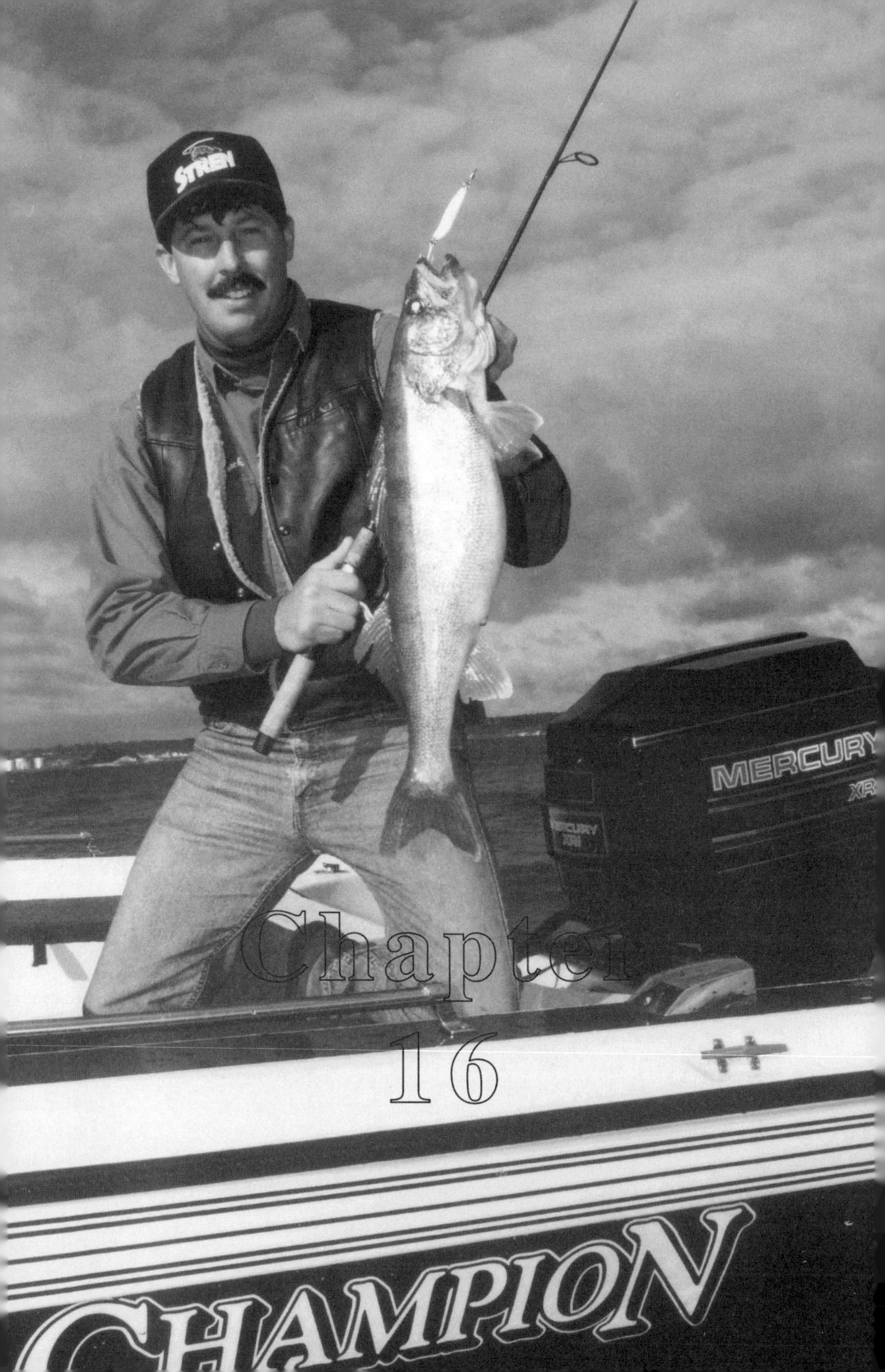

Chapter 16

Casting and Vertical Jigging Spoons

Sometimes walleye need to be spoon fed; jigging spoons that is. Pigeonholed as an ice fishing lure, jigging or slab style spoons are deadly open water lures. Casted into position or fished vertically spoons are powerful tools for deep water walleye fishing.

The jigging spoon is a versatile lure that brings a lot to the party. Their wide range of sizes allows them to be easily fished near bottom in 20 to 50 feet of water. Available in almost every shape conceivable spoons feature a wide variety of wobbling actions that are tough to top. If all this isn't enough these overlooked lures also feature a healthy dose of fish attracting color and flash.

This stated, it's not hard to see why jigging spoons work so well on walleye. What's hard to understand is why so few anglers take advantage of the action and fish catching ability these heavy weight spoons sport.

SPOON SPOTS

In natural lakes, reservoirs and the Great Lakes walleye are frequent residents of hard bottom structure. Deep water reefs or sunken islands that top out in 10 or more feet of water constitute

(Left) Jigging spoons aren't just for ice fishing. Spoons are an excellent alternative to jigs or crankbaits.

prime walleye real estate. The larger the structure the more likely it will consistently hold catchable numbers of fish.

Walleye may be holding on top of the structure, scattered along the break leading to deep water or relating to the transition where the bottom and the emerging structure meet. Jigging spoons are an ideal lure when casted to fish on top of the structure, worked down the break or jigged vertically for fish relating to the deep water transition area.

Jigging spoons are effective lures for structure fishing, but they can also be deadly when walleye set up housekeeping on the open water flats. Mud flats ranging from 20-50 feet deep attract walleye like boys to a construction site. Flats often hold walleye in summer, throughout the fall, into winter and right up until the fish move shallow in spring to spawn. In Great Lakes waters like Lake Erie, after spawning the big females again visit the deep water flats to feed and recuperate from spawning.

The best flats are those found on lakes featuring a healthy population of soft rayed bait fish like shad, alewives, emerald shiners, ciscoes or white suckers. Walleye cruise the mud flats feeding on these protein rich forage fishes. Lakes with primarily hard ray forages such as yellow perch, bluegills or darters rarely support a mud bite. These small fishes tend to stay in areas with hard bottoms or among weed cover, forcing walleye to follow suit.

Drifting and vertical jigging with spoons is an excellent way to fish the flats. This style of fishing calls for a couple pieces of specialized fishing equipment.

A set of drift socks or sea anchors are must items for controlling drifting speed. Two small to medium sized bags provides more flexibility than one large bag.

Quality drift bags feature two ropes. One rope is used to attach the bag near the transom or bow of the boat and the second rope used to turn the bag inside out when it's time to pull the bags and make another drift. If a drift sock only has one rope, they can be very difficult to pull in when full of water.

Spoons can be fished vertical or cast like jigs. The difference is spoons are usually fished with a more aggressive jigging stroke.

The wide open flats are normally featureless and shoreline sightings of little help when trying to stay on fish. A Global Positioning System (GPS) is a navigation aid that takes the guess work out of fishing for these open water walleye. GPS navigation systems operate by monitoring a number of satellites orbiting the Earth and using complicated formulas to triangulate position on Earth. If this all sounds like something out of Star Trek, don't be intimidated. GPS units are very easy to use and are capable of providing the angler with amazing navigation accuracy.

One of the most popular units with walleye anglers, the Lowrance LMS 350A is both a sonar and GPS navigation system. By using the split screen feature anglers can monitor both the graph and GPS plotter screen at the same time.

A high resolution graph, the 350A easily marks walleye holding tight to bottom in deep water. To achieve maximum power from the unit, put the graph on manual and turn up the sensitivity until light clutter begins to mark on the screen. If the screen is perfectly clear the sensitivity may not be high enough to mark fish holding tight to bottom.

This type of high resolution sonar is invaluable for locating walleye living on deep water flats. Locating fish on large flats may require a little searching. Cruise slowly and monitor the graph while hunting for schools of wandering walleye.

When fish are located mark their location using the icon or electronic marker buoy feature of the GPS unit. The icon may be a fish or any number of other symbols and will show up on the plotter screen to provide a point of reference.

Using the icon as a guide, motor a short distance directly upwind and set up a drift that will guide the boat into the fish. Like the screen of an Etch-A-Sketch the boat leaves a dotted plot trail as it moves. If the boat starts to drift off course, the plot trail makes it easy to see which way the boat needs to be moved to get back on course.

A gasoline or electric motor is used to push or pull the boat back on track as necessary. Monitoring the plot trails during repeated drifts enables an angler to make several short passes over a school of fish with deadly accuracy. The plot trails also give anglers reference so they can cover a flat throughly by making parallel drifts when trying to relocate a school of walleye that may be wandering.

As fish are caught save an icon to represent the location of landed fish. A detailed picture of the fishing situation soon begins to develop. Icons show the location of fish concentrations while plot trails indicate where the boat has traveled and waters already fished.

A WORD ON PRESENTATIONS

When casting a jigging spoon allow the bait to sink on a slack line until it hits bottom. Reel up the slack line until the weight of the spoon can be felt in the rod tip.

With the rod in the three o'clock position, lift the spoon off bottom with a pumping or pulling motion and stop the rod when it reaches the two o'clock position. Stopping the rod during the pumping action causes the spoon to pendulum towards the angler on a taunt line. Repeat this procedure until the lure is directly beneath the boat.

Maintaining slight tension in the line makes it easier to detect subtle strikes. Keeping tension in the line also allows the angler to control the fall of the lure and the wobbling action.

By switching between thin (8-10 pound test) and heavier (12-17 pound test) monofilament the angler can further influence the hang time or descent of the spoon. Thinner lines allow the spoon to fall more quickly and with a pronounced wobbling action. Heavier monofilament has more drag in the water, causing the spoon to fall slower and with a subdued wobble.

The shape of the spoon used also has a strong influence on hang time and lure action. Compact jigging spoons like the Luhr Jensen Crippled Herring sink quickly with only a moderate wobble. Wider spoons like the Mepps Syclops or Fred Arbogast Doctor Spoon displace more water causing them to sink much slower and with a pronounced side to side wobble.

When vertical jigging with spoons the action of the lure can be controlled by allowing the bait to fall on a slack or taunt line. If the lure is allowed to free fall, the spoon will give off maximum wobbling action and flash. Dropping the spoon back to bottom on a taunt line slows down the lure descent and yields a more subtle wobble.

The hang time and action of the spoon can also be influenced by adding a plastic body, pork trailer or live minnow to the treble hook. Plastic spinnerbait trailers and pork rind are durable and stay on the hook even during aggressive jigging strokes. These trailers can be soaked in fishing scent to further enhance their fish catching ability.

When dressing a jigging spoon with a live minnow hook the bait through the lips and use a subtle to moderate jigging motion to avoid tearing off the bait. Certain minnows like emerald and golden shiners are poor choices for using with jigging spoons. The delicate mouth of these minnows makes it impossible to keep bait on the hook. Minnows with tough rubber-like mouths including fatheads, suckers and chubs make excellent bait for jigging spoons.

Adding a trailer or live bait to a jigging spoon helps to bulk up the lure and make it more visible in stained or off color water. When a trailer or live bait is added to a spoon the profile of the lure also changes, giving the bait a whole new look and action in the water.

Bulking up jigging spoons is a good way to tempt fall walleye that are looking for a larger meal. During fall walleye and other predatory fish seek out larger meals that help them build a fat layer for the lean months of winter. Bulking up is also helpful when fishing in dirty water. The larger size of a bulked up spoon is easier for walleye to spot and catch in these fishing conditions.

SPOONIN' GEAR

Fishing with jigging spoons requires rods and reels that are more likely to be associated with bass than walleye fishing. The ideal spoon jigging combination is a medium action graphite baitcasting rod and reel loaded with eight to 17 pound test monofilament. Straight handle rods such as those commonly used to throw spinnerbaits or plastic worms provide a secure grip and ample room when two hands are needed to enhance an aggressive jigging action.

Jigging spoons are best attached to the business end of a line using a sturdy snap. A snap makes it easy to change lure size, brand or color and reduces line abrasion and break-offs associated with tying direct.

When selecting spoons, keep in mind that like crankbaits different models have different actions. An assortment of spoons ranging in size from 1/4 ounce to two ounces will fill most walleye fishing needs.

Some of the time tested walleye jigging spoons include Luhr Jensen's Crippled Herring and Krocodile, Little Bay de Noc's Swedish Pimple, Hopkin's Shortie, Mepps Scylops and the Blue Fox Pixee. New comers worth mention include Rapala's Treble Spoon, Bait Rigs Willow Spoon and Fish World, Inc., 3D Photo-Spoon.

SPOON MODIFICATIONS

Rigging slab style spoons for success starts with the hooks. Many models come equipped with a single hook. Other spoons feature heavy duty treble hooks like those normally used on salmon lures.

A round bend style treble hook is ideal for use with jigging spoons. The thin wire of these hooks penetrates easily into the tough mouth of a walleye.

For a little extra pocket change anglers can replace existing hooks with premium trebles that are razor sharp from tip to barb. The VMC Cone Cut, Heddon Excalibur, Owner Tournament and Mustad Triple Grip deliver the ultimate in penetration and holding power.

In areas where snags become a serious problem, a weedless treble hook can be substituted. Another option is to switch to heavier fishing line that enables the angler to straighten out snagged round bend hooks. Bent hooks can be quickly reshaped with a pair of needle nose pliers, resharpened and put back into service.

Spoon colors and flash can also be easily modified. Adding a strip of adhesive backed flash tape is the easiest way to change spoon color or add extra flash. Spoons can also be custom painted to specific needs or tastes as the angler dictates.

SPOONS & THE SUPER BRAIDS

Walleye anglers are quickly discovering the benefits of the new super braids. The thin diameter and low stretch properties of braided lines makes them ideal for jigging up deep water walleye.

Line stretch associated with monofilament can make it difficult to feel bottom, detect strikes and achieve positive hook sets when fishing in deep water. Think of your fishing line as a rubber band and you'll have a good idea how monofilament reacts when wet.

Braided lines have minimal stretch to rob the angler of feel and hook setting ability. The major brands, Stren Powerbraid, Berkley FireLine and Spiderwire, are also available in low visibility colors that disappear under water for maximum fishing success.

Jigging spoons produce walleye at any time of the year. Now's the perfect time to collect up those Dusty spoons, sharpen some hooks and head to a favorite walleye lake. Once walleye are located teaching them to eat from a spoon is the easy part!

In chapter 17 we'll entertain some traditional and unique ways to fish trolling spoons. A technique limited mostly to the Great Lakes, trolling spoons are nonetheless a deadly way to catch walleye.

CHAPTER TIPS

1. Jigging spoons work on walleye during all four seasons. Every walleye angler should keep a few of these weighted spoons handy on every fishing trip.

2. Jigging spoons bring flash, color and action to the party. For best results spoons should be fished using an aggressive popping action that allows the spoon to free fall on slack line.

3. Attach jigging spoons to fishing line using a small cross-lok style snap that makes it easy to change spoons.

4. Line size can influence spoon action. Light lines allow spoons to fall quickly and with maximum wobble. Heavier lines cause spoons to sink a little slower and with a more subtle wobble.

5. Spoons can be fished using both spinning and baitcasting equipment, but most anglers favor a six to seven foot triggerstick, baitcasting reel and 10-17 pound test monofilament.

6. The new superbraid lines are an excellent choice when spoon jigging in deep water.

Chapter 17

Spoon Trolling

Downriggers, diving planers and trolling spoons. When anglers reach for these fishing accessories they usually have salmon, steelhead or lake trout in mind. Many anglers don't realize these same tools have a home on walleye boats too. The similarities between angling tactics designed for salmon and those for walleye are astonishing. With a few minor modifications and attitude adjustment or two, anglers can tap into Great Lakes walleye fishing they never dreamed possible.

The walleye population of the Great Lakes has exploded in recent years. Excellent fishing is available throughout Lake Erie, the shoreline of Lake Huron from the Port Huron north to Alpena harbors walleye, as does much of Lake Ontario and isolated ports along the Lake Michigan shoreline.

Collectively these fisheries may contain more walleye than all the other waters in the Midwest combined! A strong statement, but one that's backed up by the walleye population estimates published by the Ohio Sea Grant. An estimated population of 50 million walleye live in Lake Erie alone, and noone knows for sure how many fish these other waters support. One thing is for sure, the walleye population is huge, the waters vast and trolling is the only practical way of fishing.

(Left) Trolling spoons is largely a Great Lakes presentation. Spoons can be trolled faster than other lures making them a great tool when covering water and hunting for fish.

SPOON TROLLING BASICS

A trolling milestone is reached once the water temperature hits 50 degrees. While walleye are often caught trolling in colder water, this water temperature represents a good starting point for spoon trolling. The very design of spoons demands that these lures be trolled faster than crankbaits or spinners to achieve their fish catching action. Typical spoon trolling speeds begin at 2 mph and range to 3 or even 4 mph at times.

The faster trolling speeds used with spoons are a dramatic advantage when trolling large open waters. Simply stated, trolling quickly covers more water in less time and puts the angler's lures in contact with the maximum number of fish. With lure speeds like these it's generally accepted that the spoon bite is a warm water presentation.

It's during this warm water period that anglers are likely to find as many Great Lakes walleye suspended in the water column as living on bottom. Suspended fish are often very active, striking savagely at spoons trolled with the help of downriggers.

"There's a trick to catching walleye on downriggers," says Larry Hartwick of Riviera Downriggers. "The mistake many anglers make is they run too many riggers at once. Walleye are more likely to be spooked by the sound of multiple downrigger cables cutting through the water than salmon. When fishing walleye, two riggers mounted at the corners of the boat is ideal."

For most walleye fishing applications two manual riggers with 24 inch arms is adequate. The Riviera Model 500 riggers on my boat have provided years of trouble free service. The nice thing about Riviera riggers is the large reel that picks up approximately two foot of cable per handle turn. Also, because these trolling aids are manufactured in Port Austin, Michigan, service and parts are readily available as needed.

Spoons and downriggers are as inseparable as the jig and minnow. Deadly on Great Lakes walleye, spoons used for trolling come in two styles. Lightweight models often referred to as flutter spoons should be fished on short leads behind the

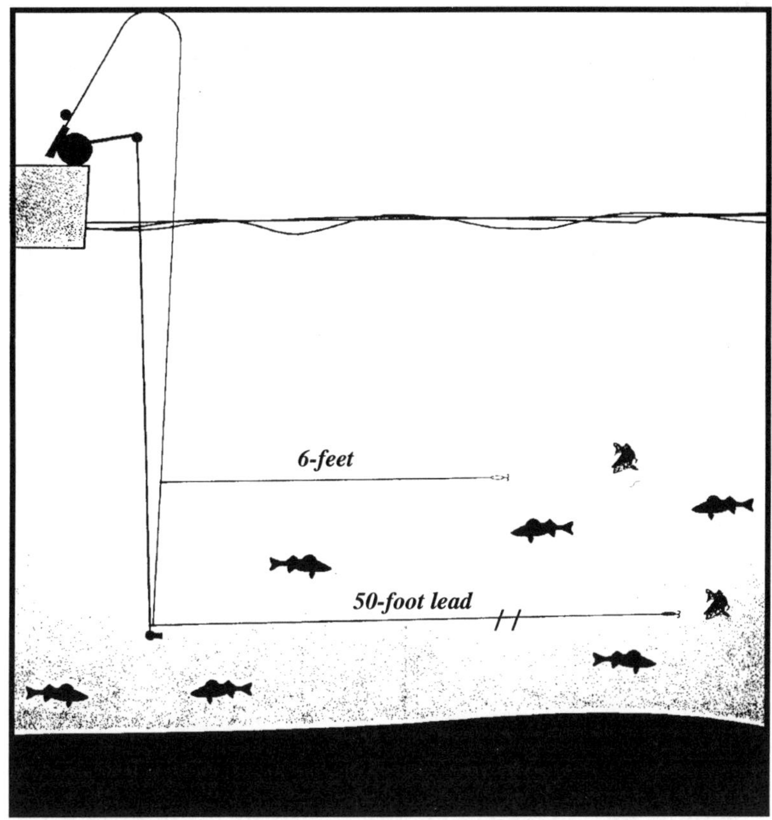

Downriggers are one of the most popular ways to fish trolling spoons. When using riggers two spoons can be fished off one line by using a slider or add-a-line.

downrigger weight. A trolling lead of 10-20 feet helps these lures achieve their maximum wobbling action. If too long a lead is used, the action of these lightweights changes from a darting wobbling action that hammers fish to a side-to-side sashay that triggers few strikes.

Spoons like crankbaits are speed sensitive. The best way to determine adequate trolling speed with spoons is to drag the lure at boat side and adjust the trolling speed until the spoon wobbles nicely.

Examples of excellent flutter type trolling spoons include the Fred Arbogast Thin Doctor, Wolverine Silver Streak, Pro Spoon,

Luhr Jensen Diamond King and Stinger. Each of these lures are walleye producers when fished on short leads in combination with downriggers. The best choices for walleye trolling are the small and medium sizes. Most anglers avoid the magnum sized spoons when trolling for walleye.

Heavier spoons double as both trolling and casting models. Often overlooked as an option for downrigger trolling, these spoons can be fished using much longer trolling leads without sacrificing lure action. Many times a longer lead will produce better, especially if walleye are spooky or reluctant to bite.

Trolling leads ranging from 50-150 feet bring a whole new dimension to downrigger trolling. Some excellent spoons to try in this category include the Luhr Jensen Krocodile, Acme Little Cleo, Blue Fox Pixie, Fred Arbogast Big Doctor and Eppinger Dardevle.

It's possible to mix up both types of spoons in the same trolling pattern. An angling technique known as a fixed slider or add-a-line enables two lures to be run off one fishing line. Rigging up this two lure trolling system is easy.

Select a heavy casting style spoon and set the bait 50 or more feet behind the boat. Attach the line into a pinch pad style downrigger release. The Off Shore Tackle OR4 light tension release is ideal for walleye fishing. Designed to provide enough tension for solid hooksets, this release can also be used effectively with light line.

Once the line is placed in the downrigger release, lower the ball 5 to10 feet into the water and prepare to attach an add-a-line leader. The add-a-line I recommend is simple to rig and highly effective. Select an Off Shore Tackle OR14 adjustable planer board release, two ball bearing swivels and about six feet of 15-20 pound test monofilament. Place the monofilament through the hole in the back of the OR14 and tie a ball bearing swivel to both ends. Attach a flutter spoon to one end of the leader and clip the other swivel over the fishing line. Complete the add-a-line by pinching the OR14 onto the main line.

Here's how the system works. Lower the add-a-line into the water making sure the spoon is working properly, then position the rod in the rod holder and reel up slack line until the rod has a nice bend in it. The OR14 holds the add-a-line right where you put it, making it possible to fish precise depth levels with ease. When a fish strikes the add-a-line the release tension insures a solid hook set. During the fight, the add-a-line will gradually slide down the line until it reaches the main spoon.

This fixed add-a-line system works much better than free moving sliders. When a fish hits a slider, there's no tension on the fish to insure a hookset. By the time the fish pulls the slider down to the main spoon, in most cases the fish is off.

Downrigger style rods are the best choice for fishing spoons with riggers. The ideal rod should be made of fiberglass or a graphite/fiberglass composite. Choose models that are seven to eight feet long with a medium action and match them to baitcasting or level wind reels capable of handling 200 yards of 10-15 pound test line.

Downrigger fishing is hard on fishing line. An abrasion resistant line with a moderate amount of stretch such as Stren's High Impact is ideal for downrigger fishing. Also, I'd recommend using a little heavier line than used for other trolling applications. Line diameter has little impact on spoon fishing success, therefore I'd suggest using at least 12 pound test. I personally use my downrigger rods and reels for both walleye and Great Lakes salmon and trout. My reels are loaded with 17 pound High Impact.

TROLLING WITH DIPSY DIVERS

Diving planes such as the famous Dipsy come into their own during the heat of summer when walleye suspend from 20-60 feet below the surface. The diver attaches to the main line and a short leader is rigged to the back of the diver. A spoon is the most common lure used with divers and both flutter and heavy casting models can be used effectively.

Dipsy divers operate using a very simple design. A wire arm

on the Dipsy is snapped into special slot. When trolled, water is forced against the surface of the diver causing it to dive. In addition to diving below the surface a Dipsy has several settings on the bottom that enable the diver to run to the right or left of the boat. The settings are 0,1,2 &3 right and 0, 1, 2, 3 left. The larger the number setting selected the further to the side the diver will run.

Keep in mind when fishing a Dipsy that if the unit is set to run to the side it won't dive as deeply as when rigged to dive straight down. As with other trolling devices the longer the lead used, the deeper the diver will run below the surface.

The book Precision Trolling features two charts that clearly show how deep the two common sizes of Dipsy divers run when fished on 20 pound test line. This data is based on actual observation by a scuba diver and includes all the settings. Copies of Precision Trolling are available for $19.95, plus shipping. Call 1-800-353-6958 to order.

When a fish hits a spoon rigged behind a Dipsy, the arm pulls free of the slot allowing the angler to simply reel in the diver and fish together. Once the fish is landed the diver can be reset in seconds, making them one of the most efficient methods of trolling available.

Divers perform best when trolled at speeds between 2-3.5 MPH. Special rods designed to handle divers are highly recommended. Most of these rods are nine to 10 feet long with an action capable of handling 20-40 pound test line.

When choosing a reel for a diver rod the classic Daiwa 47LC line counter reel is considered the standard all other reels are compared to. These high quality reels offer excellent drag systems and a dependable line clicker for setting lines, plus they hold up to 280 yards of 20 pound test monofilament.

The smaller 27LC can also be used for diver fishing, especially if thin super braid lines are used. Many anglers swear by super braids for diver trolling, stating that they get extra depth from the diver, better hookup ratios and it's easier to trip the diver when changing lures or pulling lines. If braided lines are used, select a product that's at least 20 pound test.

When fishing a diver, the rule of thumb is to select a lead length that is equal to or slightly less than the rod length. Tie up extra leaders ahead of time using a swivel on both ends and store them on a chunk of foam until they are needed.

When trolling spoons on riggers or Dipsy Divers always use a quality ball bearing snap swivel at the terminal end. Taking this one simple step will improve your spoon fishing success two fold. Ball bearing snaps cost a little more, but they allow the lure to have free movement and guarantee you won't have to deal with line twist problems.

SPOON COLOR

Spoons like crankbaits come in every color under the rainbow. I chuckle at the creative names that spoon manufacturers come up with to describe their unique color patterns. Names such as Wonder Bread, Watermelon, Dr. Death and Monkey Puke are just a few of the popular colors you'll hear anglers talking about.

I personally like spoons that feature a genuine silver or gold plate finish dressed with a little paint or flash tape. Silver and gold plate are many times brighter than nickel or brass and provide a lot more fish attracting flash in the water.

Keep in mind when you're fishing spoons you're trolling fast, covering water quickly and triggering reactionary strikes. The most effective lures are almost certain to be those fish can see the furthest.

A WORD ON SAFETY

No discussion of open water trolling would be complete without a few words of caution and common sense. The waters of the Great Lakes can provide wonderful fishing opportunities and they can also turn ugly in the blink of an eye. If you've never been caught on open water in rough seas, consider yourself lucky. I've seen expensive walleye boats pounded into pieces by huge waves, boats capsized and anglers thrown overboard. Aside from the obvious things such as a fire extinguisher and life vests, if you intend to fish the Great Lakes don't leave the dock without a dependable VHF marine radio, a GPS navigation unit, a flare gun and an anchor heavy enough to anchor even in tough conditions.

A marine radio is your life link to land. Both hand-held and permanent mounts are available. The permanent mounts require an antenna be mounted to the boat, but they provide a much wider use range than hand-helds. For my money a permanent model with a good eight foot antenna is the best choice. Marine radio signals are based on line-of-sight. In other words, the taller your antenna the further you can broadcast and receive radio signals. Also, most good marine radios have a weather ban that's invaluable for fishing the Great Lakes.

When most fishermen buy a GPS unit they are purchasing it to help mark the location of fish and bottom structure so they can return to the area on future fishing trips. The most valuable function of a GPS unit has nothing to do with fishing. A GPS unit indicates your exact location. In the event of an emergency providing the Coast Guard or other rescue workers your exact location makes for a speedy rescue. Without GPS coordinates, it could be a long wait for help.

GPS units are available in hand-held and permanent mount versions ranging in price from $200.00 to $1,000.00.

A flare gun, not just hand-held flares should be on every boat that ventures onto the Great Lakes. With a flare gun signals can be seen many times farther. Don't kid yourself, a flare gun may cost a little more, but it could be the difference between life and death.

The final piece of equipment every Great Lakes boater needs is a heavy anchor and enough line to anchor securely. In rough seas a boat can drift an amazing distance in a short time, making it difficult for rescue workers to locate and help you. Anchoring simply increases the likelihood of being found quickly. The rule of thumb to follow when anchoring is to use four times as much line as the water is deep. Attach the anchor to the bow of the boat and sit tight to wait for help.

The practice of trolling spoons is largely limited to Great Lakes waters. However, when used in the right element, few lures can match the fish catching ability of a spoon.

In chapter 18 float fishing will be the center of discussion. Floats are an ideal way to fish heavy cover such as submerged wood and weeds.

Trolling spoons come in a wide variety of shapes and actions.

Chapter 18

Fishing Bobbers In Wood & Weeds

Sometimes the best walleye fishing system isn't the most popular or the most flashy technique. The ordinary slip bobber is one of the best ways to catch walleye, especially when these sought after fish turn up in heavy weeds or submerged wood cover.

Slip floats have been around a long time and for the most part anglers still think of them as kids toys. Nothing could be further from the truth. I got my introduction to slip floats many years ago while fishing steelhead on the Little Manistee River.

The run I selected to fish was littered with broken rock, waterlogged timber and roots from trees growing along the bank. Every time I casted a traditional bottom bumping rig baited with spawn, the rig snagged and had to be broken off. Frustrated to say the least, I was sitting on the bank tying up another bottom rig, when an angler walked up, stepped into the water and made a cast. I didn't even look up figuring he would be sitting next to me any second rerigging.

The splash of a leaping steelhead brought me to attention. The silvery bullet jumped several times before the angler worked him to shore, unhooked and released the fish.

It wasn't until the fish had been released that I noticed my

(Left) Les Campbell caught this "eye" with the help of a bobber and jig combination.

neighbor was using a slip bobber with a spawn sac dangling a couple feet below. Curious, I watched as he made another cast. The float quickly righted itself and began to drift with the current. The tiny float hadn't drifted 10 feet when it tipped on its side and went under. I heard the line snap tight and a second fish bolted out of the water.

Caught flat footed, I had no recourse but to give up my spot, hike back to the truck and head into town to visit the bait shop. I purchased a few bobbers, some bobber stops and a package of split shot and was back on the water within an hour.

When I reached the water I tipped my cap to the angler who had given me a fishing lesson and made my way upstream to another hole that routinely held fish. My first cast produced a silver bullet of my own. Since that day I've used slip bobbers frequently for steelhead, walleye and many other species.

When walleye fishing in weeds or submerged wood, slip bobbers are one of my favorite and most productive ways to tempt fish from cover. The slip bobber rig I used for weed walleye is a little different than ones used to catch steelhead.

I set up a slip bobber by first selecting a 7 foot medium or medium/light action spinning rod. A slightly longer rod than used for jigging is needed for bobber fishing. Longer rods make it easier to cast in windy conditions and they help to mend line (keep extra line out of the water) when drifting a float.

This rod and reel combination is best loaded with low memory line such as Stren Easy Cast or Magna Thin. The ideal choice for float fishing is six to eight pound test.

A cloth type bobber stop is threaded onto the line, pulled up tight and the tag ends trimmed short. Next a small plastic bead is threaded onto the line, followed by a pencil or oval shaped float. I personally prefer floats that have a counter balance weight attached directly to the float. This weight makes it easier to cast the float and requires the angler to use less weight on the line. At the terminal end a small (1/32 to 1/16 ounce) jig completes the rig.

It's important to select a jig that features an eye tie coming out the top. This line tie configuration insures that the jig will rest horizontal in the water. I also look for jigs that feature thin wire hooks that are easily bend out and recovered if the jig snags.

I use a jig instead of a single hook, because the weight of the jig helps to pin the bait in one spot. When fishing in heavy weeds or wood, a frisky minnow or leech that has too much freedom of movement can easily wrap the line around weed stems or brush. The weight of the jig also works to counter balance the float, eliminating the need for split shot or other weight on the line.

Usually when I'm fishing this type of cover I'm making short casts to pockets or openings in the cover. I position myself on the raised bow platform in my boat and use the electric motor to silently scoot around looking for likely spots.

A good pair of sunglasses is vital to this fishing technique. If you can't see into the water, locating the nooks and pockets that hold fish is very difficult. I also like to be on the water early if I expect to fish floats. Early in the morning the water is usually calm, making it easier to see under the surface.

Both minnows and leeches make good live bait for this style of fishing. Crawlers don't have as much action and they tend to attract the wrong kinds of fish such as bluegills, yellow perch, rock bass and other small fish.

A durable minnow such as a fathead, dace or chub is my first choice. These hearty minnows can be casted many times before the bait must be replaced. Also, minnows are the least likely bait to be bothered by unwanted fish species.

Leeches are more readily available during the summer months and they have a built in wiggle that walleye simply can't resist. Unfortunately, other less desirable fish also share the same attraction to this bait. I use a medium or large size leech to discourage bluegill, crappie and other panfish from biting.

The techniques used to fish both weeds and wood are similar. However, weed areas tend to be sprawling flats that are difficult to cover completely. Not surprisingly, weed fishing can be a slow and tedious way of tempting walleye. Not every clump of aquatic growth is going to harbor a walleye. The angler's job is to fish every likely looking spot in hopes of locating those in use by walleye.

Walleye are attracted to a wide variety of weeds, but common pond weed or what is often called cabbage is an ideal cover for walleye. Pond weed tends to grow in deeper water than most other aquatic plants. In clear water environments these towering weed stalks often thrive in water up to 10-15 feet deep.

Another advantage of cabbage weed is the way this plant grows. Usually found growing in clumps, clusters and loose groupings, walleye select this type of cover because it provides enough shade and shelter to make them feel comfortable. At the same time cabbage weed is usually sparse enough that walleye are able to easily swim among the stalks while hunting for bait fish, aquatic insects and other forage.

Unlike bass that are built to hunt in weeds, walleye are more suited as an open water predator. Readily adapted to hunting in sparse weed cover, walleye fare much poorer when faced with dense weed growth. When the aquatic weeds are dense, walleye are most likely to be found hunting the edges. When the cover is scattered, walleye cruise throughout the cover in search of food.

It's difficult to predict which depth level walleye will be located at, however it's a safe bet that the deeper weeds are a good place to start. This is especially true if northern pike are abundant in the area. Northerns tend to dominate the weeds, forcing walleye and other smaller fish to the weed edges.

When I'm looking for walleye in weeds, areas where the aquatic growth tapers off quickly into deep water are usually the most productive. Walleye feel more secure when a deep water sanctuary is nearby. Also, weed edges tend to funnel movements of baitfish within reach of waiting walleye.

It would be nice if walleye scattered uniformly throughout weed flats. Unfortunately, certain features within the weeds that only the walleye seem to understand tend to concentrate fish in clusters. The only way to find these hot pockets is the old fashioned way, by working at it.

Fishing walleye in submerged timber is very similar to fishing in weeds, except that much of the action takes place near shore. For the most part you're looking for trees that have washed into the water or been blown down by wind storms. Beavers are another source of submerged timber. The fallen timber these tireless workers are responsible for can be a real bonanza to walleye fishing.

Regardless of how the timber got into the water, it is usually located near shallow water. This simple fact means that walleye using submerged timber as cover will be easily spooked.

When you fish timber, a quiet approach is absolutely critical. Cut your outboard motor a couple hundred yards short of the area to be fished and use a silent electric motor to move the boat into position.

Timber fishing is also best early and late in the day when light levels are low. As the sun rises, abandon spots that are in the direct sunlight and concentrate on timber that's in the shade.

Not surprisingly the best lakes for timber fishing are remote waters with few cottages and limited boat traffic. The more quiet the lake is, the better chance that walleye will use shallow areas with submerged timber.

Beaver can be a walleye fisherman's best friend. Not only do beavers topple trees into the water, but they also cut and store limbs and branches near their lodges as a winter food source. These dense collections of brush are real magnets for minnows and ultimately walleye.

The submerged brush around a beaver lodge can often be so dense it's even tough to fish with a slip bobber rig. If the timber is very dense, it's a good idea to substitute the jig for a weedless single hook such as a Eagle Claw 249WA in size No. 4. This hook can be fished among brush that would be otherwise impossible to fish.

Fishing timber also requires good sunglasses and it helps to fish from the elevated platform of a boat. From this vantage point it's easier to see into the water and identify pockets and openings among the timber.

Fishing slip bobbers in weeds and submerged timber is neither flashy nor traditional, but this unique angling method is effective. Most anglers ignore these areas because fishing is difficult. Yes, it's true fishing weeds and wood is a little more work. Of course when you catch these fish, the satisfaction is also sweeter.

In the next chapter we'll look at a more traditional form of float fishing, casting slip bobbers to rock structure.

CHAPTER TIPS

1. Floats can be used after dark by simply sliding a piece of surgical tubing over the stem of the float and inserting a small cylume stick. A cylume stick will glow brightly for several hours making it easy to see your floats even in the gloom of night.

2. Foam and balsa wood floats both work equally well. Foam floats are less expensive, but the wooden versions tend to hold up to rough treatment a little better.

3. Float fishing takes patience. Fish slowly and throughly when fishing cover such as weeds and wood.

The modern slip float is a serious walleye fishing tool.

Chapter 19

Fishing Bobbers On Rock

In some parts of walleye country fishing rock covered reefs with slip bobbers is a way of life. In others you almost never see this angling technique practiced.

One thing about fishing that has always amazed me is how certain angling techniques become localized and rarely used outside a region. This is especially apparent with slip bobbers. Literally thousands of anglers who fish natural lakes throughout Minnesota and northern Wisconsin swear by this angling technique, yet you rarely see it practiced in other parts of walleye wonderland.

Part of my motivation for doing this book was to expose anglers to other forms of walleye fishing and help folks master as many techniques as possible. When it comes to fishing slip bobbers, it's hard to find an easier technique to master and one that's more efficient.

Think about it. With most forms of walleye fishing a degree of inefficiency always looms over the presentation. Use jigs or rigs as an example. Jigs and other bottom fishing rigs are forever snagging on bottom and lost. Valuable fishing time is wasted while another lure or rig is tied on and baited.

Slip floats position the bait above bottom where it is easier for walleye to see and catch, snags are far and few between and

(Left) The author took this walleye from one of the many spawning reefs near Port Clinton, OH.

when a bite occurs you don't have to be a fishing expert to recognize it! That's the beauty of slip bobbers. They are among the most efficient and easy to use bait delivery systems a walleye angler can choose from.

So why are slip bobbers popular in some areas and not in others. Who knows? But I do know that those anglers who have taken the time to learn bobber fishing aren't about to quit using them.

Slip floats are a great way to fish shallow water structure such as rock reefs, sand bars, points, sunken islands and the saddles that form between these spots. While many anglers might argue that casting a jig or crankbait could be just as effective, a bobber rig brings a whole new element and presentation to fishing structure.

When fishing a float the bait is suspended just off bottom and drifted or casted into position. Usually a very active bait such as a minnow or leech produces best. Nightcrawlers can also be effective.

Using slip floats provides the angler with more control of the bait. Or in other words the bait is positioned where a fish can eat it longer. Also, the fact that the bait is presented slowly increases the likelihood of interesting both active and inactive fish. Other lures such as crankbaits or spinners appeal mostly to active fish.

The necessary equipment for fishing floats is pretty straight forward. A spinning rod that's 6.5 to 7 foot long and a lightweight spinning reel spooled with six or eight pound test line is a good place to start. The rod need not be an expensive graphite model. In fact, many anglers prefer fiberglass rods for fishing bobbers because the softer action makes it easier to cast accurately. Also, fiberglass or graphite/fiberglass composite rods are far less expensive than high modulus graphite.

A cloth knot style bobber stop is threaded onto the line, pulled up tight and the tag ends clipped off. My experience with various styles of bobber stops suggests that the knot type are the most durable and functional. Others are either difficult to put on the line, they wear out quickly or they catch in the rod guides when casting.

After the bobber stop is installed, a small bead is threaded onto the line, followed by the float of choice. These days there are more floats to choose from than places to fish. The European style wooden floats have become very popular, yet these fishing aids cost about two or three times as much as similar models made of foam. Both types will work well. The pencil or oval shaped floats are the best choice for walleye fishing.

A split shot or two is used to counter-balance the float and at the terminal end a wide bend or Kahle style hook is an excellent choice. Kahle style hooks are lightweight so the bait can move freely, made of thin wire that penetrates easily and the wide gap design makes it more difficult for fish to throw the hook.

When counter-balancing a float use enough weight so the float barely stays afloat. Split shots are the normal weight used to counter-balance a float. These small weights should be attached to the line approximately 12 inches above the hook.

Counter-balancing a float is important. If the float is too buoyant, walleye may feel the resistance and drop the bait before the angler has time to set the hook. Floats can be counter-balanced on the water or at home in the bath tub before leaving on a fishing trip.

Since it takes a few minutes to rig up a slip float, I'd recommend setting up two rods right away. If one rod becomes fouled, a second line is rigged and ready to go. Also, many anglers prefer to fish two rods at once where legal to increase their odds of contacting fish.

When fishing structure the boat is usually anchored in place and the float rigs casted and/or drifted into position. Many experienced float fishermen prefer to anchor off the bow and let the transom of the boat slide back and forth in the wind. When using this anchoring technique the boat is positioned well upwind of the area to be fished and the anglers fish out of the back of the boat. Anchored in this position, more anchor line can be let out as needed to cover available water throughly.

Those anglers who use this anchoring technique often carry 200 feet or more of anchor line. Depending on how deep the water is and how windy the day, it often takes 100 feet of line to hold the average walleye boat. A good rule of thumb to follow is to use at least four times as much line as the water is deep.

My anchors are equipped with at least 1/2 inch diameter soft nylon rope. I got a bargain on some used rope at an army surplus store a few years back. The rope was designed for mountain climbing and would have retailed new for around $2 a foot. I got two 100 foot coils for about $20 each and the rope was in excellent condition!

If you can find a deal like this on quality rope buy it. But even if you can't, good rope is worth the investment. While quality anchor line isn't cheap it is stronger, softer and easier to work with than the discount ropes marketed as ski tow lines.

Anchor lines should also be stored wound neatly on a "H" shaped piece of plywood or similar device designed to hold extension cords. If the anchor line isn't kept organized, it is sure to find its way into trouble.

I think of anchor lines differently than most anglers. An anchor helps you hold your boat in position to fish, but even more importantly an anchor holds your boat and prevents you from drifting aimlessly in the event of a mechanical breakdown or emergency. Your life and the life of those with you could honestly depend on the rope purchased as an anchor line.

The best anchor for all around use is a model with large flukes that dig into the bottom. The classic navy style anchor is tough to beat, but some of the new collapsible fluke style anchors are lighter and easier to store. Stay away from mushroom style anchors that are designed for small boats and soft bottom areas.

If you choose a traditional navy style anchor it will require at least 15 pounds to hold most 14-17 foot boats. I'm using a 20 pound navy to hold my 19 foot boat and there are days when I must add a five foot length of coated logging chain to insure the anchor bites securely. The chain helps to keeps the flukes digging into the bottom instead of pulling free when a wave jerks the line.

Another tip that makes anchoring easier is to mount a cleat

Floats suitable for walleye fishing come in a wide variety of sizes and shapes.

on the top deck of the boat near the bow. If you have open access to this part of your boat, bolt the cleat into place using stainless bolts with nylock nuts that won't vibrate loose over time. Trying to tie off an anchor line to the bow eye of a boat is risky business even when it's calm. Don't even try it when the waves are rolling.

People who fish floats a lot take their anchors and anchoring technique seriously. After all if the anchor won't hold, your chances of catching fish are zero.

Often the hardest part of slip bobber fishing is anchoring the boat. Once the boat is secured in position the fun can begin.

Ideally the bobber stop should be set so the bait is within a few inches of bottom. If you don't know the depth, it may take a couple casts and adjustments to get the ideal setting.

When I'm fishing reefs and other structure that's surrounded by deeper water I usually begin by working the deeper water adjacent to the structure. When walleye are inactive they usually slide down the structure towards deep water and often hole up at the point where the structure and otherwise flat bottom meet. If fish aren't encountered here, more anchor line can be let out and an effort made to fish progressively shallower water.

The windward side of any bottom structure is always a good place to start, but sometimes the wind blows in from a direction where the structure is flat or otherwise offers little interest to walleye. Sometimes the best fishing is found on the downwind side of the structure. It all depends on how the bottom structure lays out and which way the wind is blowing.

Wind makes anchoring and boat control more difficult, but it also stimulates walleye to move up onto the shallow food shelves to feed. Never fight the wind when bobber fishing. Instead, anchor so you can use the wind to drift your floats into position.

Obviously to accomplish this feat you need to know how the structure lays. Ideally you should familiarize yourself with the structure before you intend to fish it. If you're fishing a new area you may have to move the boat two, three or more times to encounter fish.

When the boat is positioned properly and walleye are within casting distance, anyone can catch these fish with a slip bobber rig. Novice anglers, kids and old pros alike can all enjoy the action. That's one of the reasons this style of fishing has become so popular in Minnesota and Wisconsin where a lot of walleye are caught by anglers who book a fishing guide. Imagine being a guide and having to teach kids and others how to effectively cast and fish jigs!

Another aspect of bobber fishing that's worth mentioning is fishing after dark. By simply taping a small light stick to the bobber or using one of the many lighted bobbers on the market, the fishing fun can continue after dark.

Fishing after sunset makes a lot of sense. The shallow water food shelves where walleye are often targeted with floats don't see a lot of walleye action when the weather is clear and calm. It takes a little wind to bring the fish up, but under the cover of darkness walleye cruise these shallows every evening hunting for food.

The odds of finding walleye at home on shallow water structure is much better at night than during the daylight hours. If you decide to fish after dark, you'll need to keep unnecessary light to a minimum. Most anglers use portable black lights mounted on the floor of the boat so they can see to tie on lures, hook baits, etc.

The most productive times to fish after dark are for a couple hours after sunset and again just before sunrise. Fishing usually slows during the middle of the night. Spring and fall are great times to take advantage of night fishing opportunities, because it gets dark so early in the evening and later in the morning.

Fishing floats over hard bottom areas is an excellent way to bring walleye and hot grease together. A third style of float fishing is rarely practiced, yet it can be one of the best ways to catch walleye in rivers. In the final chapter we'll explore the last but not least effective method of catching the popular walleye.

Chapter 20

Fishing Bobbers In Current

If there's one fishing presentation that gets lost in the walleye shuffle, fishing with floats would have to qualify. Despite the fact that floats are versatile, easy to use and effective, they are usually among the last presentation options anglers consider. This is especially true if the fishing destination is a river.

Even among those anglers who regularly fish with floats, few anglers have discovered that float fishing is one of the best ways to fish moving water. Call it tunnel vision or simple stubbornness, but most walleye anglers feel the only serious way to fish rivers is by bumping bottom with some form of live bait.

Ironically, slip bobbers are among the most efficient means of fishing live bait tight to bottom. Imagine a jig drifting along a couple inches off bottom with a lively minnow squirming and struggling to free itself. Sound like something a walleye would eat? You bet, and the amazing part is very few anglers have discovered this unique fishing method.

What's even more exciting is this particular presentation is just as effective from shore as it is from a boat. You can't say that about very many walleye fishing methods.

The slip bobber rigs and equipment used to fish rivers are

(Left) Dan Johnson chose to wade from shore for this slip bobber "eye".

similar to those used to fish weeds and submerged timber. Like all slip bobber rigs, installing a bobber stop is the first step. The cloth knot type stops are the best choice for all walleye fishing applications. These bobber stops come packaged on a piece of plastic tubing. The line is thread through the tubing and one bobber stop slid off onto the line. The knot is a fixed to the line by pulling the tag ends of the bobber stop up firmly. The tag ends are cut short and a small plastic bead is threaded onto the line, followed by the float of choice and finally with a jig at the business end.

The primary difference between slip bobber rigs used in weeds and wood and those used in current is in the size jig used at the terminal end and rod length. When fishing floats in weeds and wood the jigs selected are usually crappie sized 1/32 and 1/16 ounce models. When casting float rigs in current larger 1/8, 3/16 and 1/4 ounce jigs are required to insure the line stays vertical in the water and the bait is positioned close to bottom.

Rods designed for stream steelhead fishing are ideal for casting floats in rivers. The longer rods favored by steelhead anglers offer the walleye fisherman some clear advantages. Perhaps the most obvious advantage is the ability to make long casts. Casting distance is important because anglers are often restricted to fishing from shore or wading.

Secondly, a longer rod makes it easier to mend line (keep the line up out of the water) while the float is drifting downstream. If too much line drags in the water the float won't drift in the upright position and the bait could be lifted off bottom by water resistance pulling against the line.

This style of fishing is one example where the new super braid lines out perform ordinary monofilament. Thin, yet strong, super braid lines enable anglers to make extra long casts. Also, because braided lines are very thin and they don't absorb water like monofilament, it's easier to mend line and keep the jig drifting along near bottom. Thirdly, the low stretch characteristic of braided lines means anglers can enjoy a bone jarring hook set even when making long casts.

Braided super lines are excellent products, but a word of caution regarding these lines is in order. Because these lines have little stretch, anglers must fish with a much lighter drag setting than normal and use caution not to over-stress their expensive rods. Many a two piece rod has ended up a three piece model when an unsuspecting angler spooled up with super braid.

Monofilament can also be used effectively to cast slip floats in rivers, but anglers must be content to make shorter casts. Quality six or eight pound test line is a good choice for river fishing applications.

When casting floats in rivers the ideal places to fish are holes that feature a lazy current, long gravel or sand runs and shallow flats where the water depth varies little. Bobbers can also be used to effectively fish the spillway area below dams and in areas where the bottom is so snag littered that fishing a jig or other bottom rig is out of the question.

Areas to avoid include places where the water depth varies a great deal or where the current is very swift and or deep.

The best way to fish floats in rivers is to cast upstream and quartering slightly across the current. Fished in this manner the float drifts naturally with the flow of water for the longest distance. Standing on shore, wading or casting from an anchored boat is the best way to fish floats in current.

It usually takes a few casts to determine the ideal depth setting for the bobber stop. Keep in mind that if the jig hits bottom frequently it is likely to snag and be lost, or if the jig is positioned too far off bottom walleye will ignore the offering. Once you're convinced that the jig is drifting along within a couple inches of bottom it's time to get serious.

As the float drifts downstream keep the rod tip high to prevent line from laying on the water surface and reel up slack line as it's formed. When the bobber nears the end of its downstream drift, reel it in and make another cast upstream.

It usually takes several casts and drifts to throughly fish an area. Once an area has been fished throughly, move upstream to a new location and repeat the process.

While the float is drifting your focus should be on the bobber. Rarely does the float get plucked under water in one clean jerk, but rather the float tips on its side and then slides under water. What's happening is the walleye grabs the jig and stops its downstream movement. Meanwhile the float continues to drift downstream until the line pulls tight and the current tips the float on its side and pulls it under.

Watch the float closely and set the hook the second it tips, wobbles or shows any sign of movement. Because subtle movements of the float telegraph strikes, the best floats to use are ones that have no weight attached to the lower stem. Weighted floats ride upright in the water, giving no indication of a strike even if a fish grabs the bait momentarily.

Good float styles for river fishing include oval and pencil shapes. These floats are easy to cast and capable of handling the jig weight needed to fish effectively in current.

The jigs used for this presentation should have an eye tie that comes directly out the top. This line tie configuration keeps the bait positioned horizontally and drifting naturally in the water. Minnows, leeches and crawlers can all be used effectively as bait. For best results the bait should be lively and wiggling as much as possible.

A single hook can also be used in place of a leadhead jig. Good hooks to choose from include Kahle style wide bends, beak style and bait holder models in the No. 4 or 2 size. If a single hook is used, the bobber must be counter-balanced with split shot placed on the line about 12-inches above the hook.

As an added attractor tie a few strands of colorful yarn, crystal flash, flash-a-bou or chenille on the hook to add a visual enticement. These products are available at most sport shops catering to fly or steelhead fishermen.

Casting slip bobbers in rivers may be one of the more unusual walleye fishing methods, but it isn't without a time and place. Easier to master than jig fishing and a lot more efficient in snag filled waters, casting floats is yet another method that should be added to every walleye angler's bag of tricks.

Ultimately, that's what walleye fishing is all about. If these past 20 chapters hasn't taught you anything else, it should have taught you that there are many ways to catch walleye. No single walleye fishing method works all the time in all waters. That's the bad news. The good news is figuring out what works is more than half the fun.

CHAPTER TIPS

1. When fishing floats in current wading or casting from shore is one of the best ways to fish. You can also fish from a boat by anchoring in areas not accessible from shore.

2. The new superbraid lines work very well when casting floats from shore. The thin diameter of these lines allows anglers to cast farther and cover more water.

3. When casting floats in current, cast quartering upstream and reel up the slack line as the float drifts towards you. Keeping slack out of the line causes the float to drift better and makes for a solid hook set when the time comes.

OTHER BOOKS AVAILABLE FROM MARK ROMANACK'S OUTDOOR COMMUNICATIONS

ADVANCED WALLEYE STRATEGIES

This hard copy book is a comprehensive guide to walleye fishing. Written in 1993 **Advanced Walleye Strategies** contains 246 pages, dozens of photos and illustrations, plus a where to section that highlights some of the most productive walleye fisheries in North America. Price: $15.00 plus $4.00 shipping and handling.

PRECISION TROLLING

The bible of trolling, **Precision Trolling** contains depth diving data for over 120 crankbaits and other trolling hardware including Jet Divers, Dipsy Divers, Lead Core Line and Snap Weights. Each lure or trolling aid features a life size identification photo and easy to read graph that shows the "feet down" baits will run depending on the "feet back" or trolling lead used. The 140 page book is printed on card stock. Price: Paper versions are $20.00 plus $4.00 shipping and handling, Pro Versions are laminated and sell for $25.00 plus $4.00 shipping and handling.

BANK FISHING SECRETS

Written by Mark Romanack for noted professional fisherman Mike McClelland, **Bank Fishing Secrets** was written for anglers who enjoy fishing from shore, piers and docks. Simple and straight forward techniques are used to help anglers catch fish in rivers, lakes, ponds, reservoirs and the Great Lakes. Also included are tips for ice fishing, plus favorite recipes. Soft cover and 139 pages, this book contains dozens of photographs and illustrations, plus many color photos. Price: $15.00 plus $4.00 shipping and handling.

All books are available by sending check or money order to Outdoor Communications, 20061 21 Mile Road, Tustin, MI 49688. Orders are shipped daily.